#ChurchToo

#ChurchToo

How Purity Culture Upholds Abuse
and How to Find Healing

Emily Joy Allison

Broadleaf Books
Minneapolis

For everyone who has come forward with the truth,
and everyone within whom the truth still burns.
Me too.

CONTENTS

FOREWORD

On November 21, 2017, I was finishing a residency at St. Johns University in Minnesota. I had gone there to finish my first book.

By the time I left, I'd had my last Thanksgiving with my in-laws, then I moved out of my home and ended my twelve-year marriage.

But before all of that, I spent time going to Mass, writing, and walking through the snowy woods, trying not to pray to a God I wasn't sure I believed in anymore. During the evenings, I'd go into vespers and sit alone in the church, watching the monks, the men, go through their rituals, which seemed both so new and ancient to me, since I'd been raised evangelical. I thought, "These men cannot get me here. I am safe here."

My marriage was ending and the world was falling down around me. The #MeToo movement had begun that October and was picking up steam. Every morning, I'd read the news: another bad man outed, another woman's shame on display, another woman's strength asserted.

I, too, carried stories in my body. A boss who'd harassed me at a literary conference. My sister's abuser, who was a relative. And for me, a dorm room, two men, beer, and a memory that haunted me for years until 2017, when while watching Brett Kavanagh's confirmation hearing, I understood that it hadn't been my fault.

But on November 21, 2017, all of that was swirling through the air like the snow at St. John's, both making it so hard to breathe.

That day, checking Twitter after a day of writing, I saw the hashtag #ChurchToo. I clicked immediately and read and read. Each story pulled me down and down until I was submerged in a world of stories that were both foreign and familiar. They weren't my stories, but they were my stories.

I had been raised evangelical and homeschooled in Texas in the 1990s. There I was raised with the doctrine of baptism by full immersion. Only then would we be fully purified.

Reading the #ChurchToo thread was an immersion of another kind, a baptism in a world of truth.

Months before in couples therapy, where I was frantically trying to hold together the fraying ends of my marriage, the therapist had told my husband and me that I'd been "spiritually abused."

"Spiritual abuse is when the Bible is used to control and restrain a person," she'd explained. My husband was confused.

"Isn't that what religion is?" he'd asked.

She tried to explain. He didn't understand.

We'd gotten married at twenty-two, both of us pure until marriage. Well, pure-ish for me. There was still that night in the dorm room, which had happened when I was dating him, and I'd convinced myself it never happened. I'd pushed it from my mind, and it would only return when I'd smell Bud Light or the Clearasil face wash I'd used to clean my whole body in the shower the morning after.

Years later, I'd read about a 2013 study where 0.5 percent of women surveyed reported getting pregnant before they'd had sex. These women were more likely to have signed a "chastity pledge" and more likely to have had parents who'd had trouble discussing sex and birth control.

The study's authors were confused and thought that it was a statistical anomaly, that maybe the women had forgotten.

But to me, it made perfect sense. I'd been raised in the purity culture of the 1990s. I'd been given a ring at sixteen. I'd been told that no man would want me if I was ruined, used—like a dirty tissue, as one Sunday school teacher had demonstrated: "You are the tissue. No one wants a used tissue."

Raised to believe my body was my primary value in a marriage, I'd done everything I could to stay pure. Except one night, where there was drinking and I'd said no, but it happened anyway, and now everything I'd tried to be was lost.

I refused to let that happen. It was a conscious decision to try to forget. I could only live through denial.

If I would have been able to talk about what happened, if I would have had the language of consent, the language of boundaries and healthy sexuality, I would have been able to forge for myself a path of autonomy, one where my value wasn't my body.

When I had that language, when I finally was able to say, "I am worth more," it ended my marriage. And during that divorce, my ex tried to argue that I owed him $10,000 for his investment in my brain. That's all I was—a body. My lawyer and I laughed at that line item, which we fought against and won. But it still stands there in the spreadsheet, an accounting of my worth as a human. Brain: $10,000. Vagina?

When I left my marriage, I found a new therapist and told her about spiritual abuse, and she said, "Oh, that's just *abuse* abuse."

And that therapist was right.

And that therapist was also wrong.

The intersection of religion and sexual abuse is pervasive and insidious. As Emily Joy Allison lays out in this book, even for those not raised in conservative evangelical faith traditions, the myths of purity culture are steeped into American society.

Allison lays it out with the precision of a doctor cutting out a cancer—thanks to Bush-era policies, abstinence-only education is pervasive in schools across America. The narrative that pits fetus against human mother is one that our culture buys writ large, when in reality it's as ridiculous a premise as debating flat earth versus round.

Sexual abuse, when wrapped in the sugarcoating of religion, is a particularly toxic and American poison. It infects our society, from our state-level policies on Planned Parenthood funding, to Medicaid dollars, to school sex ed, to the availability of birth control and Supreme Court decisions on whether birth control should be covered by employers.

And in this country are powerful pockets of control—churches—unscrutinized locales of religious and patriarchal law.

If religious myths about purity and bodies are the toxins that float through our culture, poisoning our air, Emily Joy Allison's book is the antidote.

A graduate of Moody Bible Institute, Allison is a Samson breaking down the walls of an unholy temple from the inside. She writes with the understanding of someone who was raised in the prison of purity culture but from the perspective of someone who is freed.

Her perspective opens the prison door—offering an escape for people who are trapped but also inviting others in to understand an influential aspect of American culture.

#ChurchToo is an invitation to honesty. It's a baptism in truth. It's a holy reckoning. As I read it, I thought of Luke 12:2–3, which speaks of the holy justice, warning, "Nothing is covered up that will not be uncovered, and nothing secret that will not become known. Therefore whatever you have said in the dark will be heard in the light, and what you

have whispered behind closed doors will be proclaimed from the housetops."

Allison is this light. But as much as it is a condemnation, it is also an invitation to something better. Allison's work does dredge up the muck of religion, but she also offers a better way. The gospel of 1 Peter 2:9 declares that God has "called you out of darkness into his marvelous light." Whatever else this book is, it is an invitation into a marvelous light, into a world where sex is not shamed but affirmed, where gender identities are not mistakes or sins but crucial aspects of our glorious selves.

Part memoir and part manual, this book is both scalpel and bandage. It slices through the disease but also offers healing. It's the book I want to give to every pastor who refused to talk to me without my husband present, to the camp counselor who said women were like wild horses who needed to be tamed into submission, to the friends who advised my family to forgive my sister's abuser because, after all, hadn't God forgiven King David of that one sin?

This is also the book I wish I could have given to myself at eighteen, a manual unraveling all the things I had been told that were wrong, the things that would keep me tied up and wrapped up until, at thirty-three, I finally got free, not because I was so enlightened, but because I was so broken.

In the aftermath of 2017, I'd often heard arguments that #MeToo had gone too far, but I never believed it. I didn't believe it because I knew too many stories that still lay in the secret parts of so many bodies. I didn't believe it because I knew that the double layers of patriarchy and religion had yet to be fully reckoned with.

I remembered the youth pastor at the megachurch in Eden Prairie, Minnesota, who disappeared one day amid rumors he'd slept with underage students. "Slept with" as if a thirty-five-year-old pastor and a seventeen-year-old could ever have a fully consensual relationship. I remember that story so often, because at the time, my sister was being assaulted.

I wouldn't know until later, until I was in college, what had been happening, but I don't think the two are unrelated.

When abuse is treated with silence and shame, we learn to handle it with silence and shame.

When respectable men sweep crimes under the prayer rug of our churches, what they teach us is that our bodies don't matter.

But they do matter.

And #MeToo will have gone far enough when it cleans out every aspect of shame in our society.

What Allison is doing in this book is an act of grace—a holy gift to those of us broken, to those of us in shame, to those of us lost in a world that doesn't value our bodies, that turns victims into villains.

This book is calling us forth from the darkness into a light. And I hope you read it, and I hope you get free.

—*Lyz Lenz, author of* God Land: A Story of Faith, Loss and Renewal in Middle America *and* Belabored: A Vindication of the Rights of Pregnant Women

INTRODUCTION

Our bodies hold our stories. Long after the memories have become like a faded dream to our minds and hearts, our bodies remember.

My body felt like it was being forcibly shoved down memory lane on November 21, 2017, as I sat silently at my kitchen table reading the news and cupping an oversized glass of rosé between both hands to keep them from shaking. Names and faces of male celebrities whose movies I hadn't been allowed to watch growing up as a home-schooled pastor's daughter flashed across my laptop screen, and even though I didn't know these men, reading the allegations against them suddenly made me feel like I was sixteen again. I felt panicked, vulnerable. And so, so angry.

Without stopping to think too hard about my feelings, I grabbed my phone and sent a frantic group text to several friends. "Should I out my abuser on Twitter?" I wrote. "Probably, huh?" I didn't consciously know why that exact moment seemed like the right time to share a story with the entire internet that I usually reserved for close friends and therapists. I wasn't thinking about the fact that it had been ten years almost to the day since the only world I knew fell apart. November 12, 2007—just nine days before. But my body knew. And my body was ready for everyone else to know too.

Supportive texts from my friends started trickling in, and I decided to do this thing before I lost the sudden burst of courage. I took a deep breath, stood up, poured myself another glass of rosé, sat back down, and started typing:

"Hey, so. This is me being brave. This is me being brave as a result of so many women in the world being brave right now. This is me standing on your shoulders. I'm so thankful for all of you."

I was through the second glass before I'd finished sharing my story in one long thread, tweet by tweet. Details. Names. Of my abuser, of the church where he found me. Dates and places. I relived months of trauma in under an hour, feeling like I was watching my life in fast-forward. When I sent the final tweet, I stood up shakily, gripping the edge of the kitchen table for support and letting my head fall between my shoulders. *Now what?*

—

When I was abused as a teen, I didn't know it. Most of the adults in my life didn't know it either. It took years to be able to look at the trauma I had experienced and attach the word *abuse* to it, something I was only able to do after talking to a therapist in college who told me she could not believe I hadn't been sexually assaulted because I was presenting all the same behaviors and thought patterns as someone who had been. I didn't realize at the time that what was happening to me was abusive because it had been modeled to me as the ultimate fairy-tale romance my entire life.

Growing up, my parents regaled my siblings and me with retellings of their love story, how they fell in love when my father was a Southern Baptist youth pastor in a small-town church and my mother was a teen in his youth group. It was OK though, they told us, because my father was sure to ask permission from the head pastor of the church as well as my mother's parents, both of whom gave their blessing for him to date my mother, who was seven years his junior. They married just a few days after her high school graduation. I was born three years later, the first of seven children.

This was love, they told us. And if we wanted love like that, it was important that we followed all God's rules for love.

God had a lot of rules, as it turns out.

My parents kept us in the dark about sex as long as they possibly could, but when it became clear that a feature of our participation in junior high youth group at the nondenominational evangelical megachurch we had started attending would be the occasional "talk" from the youth pastor, they realized they couldn't wait much longer. The summer before I started sixth grade, my parents sat me down awkwardly in a hotel hot tub on a family road trip (a move that I think they ended up regretting, as the "sex talk" in my family came to be known euphemistically as "The Hot Tub Talk" forevermore after that) and explained the bare-bones mechanics of biological procreation, then spent the rest of the conversation stressing, in no uncertain terms, that you weren't to do that, or anything like it, until you were married, to a man, because God says so. That made sense enough to my twelve-year-old self who had just recently developed a first crush, but about a year later, my parents informed me that we'd be taking a special weekend trip, just the three of us, to talk about some more important things.

When the weekend finally came, my mother took me shopping at the mall, loading my arms up with bags and bags of trendy new school clothes. Then we went out to dinner and met up with my father, and when we got in the car, they started playing some cassette tapes from a series by Dr. James Dobson of Focus on the Family. The series was about insecurity, peer pressure, relationships, and other issues young people face as they grow up. At one point,

Dr. Dobson started talking about "masturbation"—I had only heard that word once or twice and had no idea what it meant—but they quickly fast-forwarded through that bit. By the time we reached our destination, a retreat property owned by a family friend, they were ready to educate me on exactly how much God expected of me when it came to sex.

They refreshed my memory about the talk we'd had the previous year in the hot tub. I was reminded that obviously, God forbids me from having sex before I get married. And then my father asked me about dating. "How long," he asked, "do you think you should wait to kiss a boy if you're dating?" I was too naive to realize it was a trick question, so I thought about it as genuinely as I could and gave it my best shot: "I don't know . . . a few weeks? A few months?" At thirteen, I could barely muster up the courage to speak to the boy I had a crush on, so kissing anybody was such an abstract idea.

My father laughed out loud as if he couldn't contain himself and then sobered up quickly. "Oh no, no," he said. "We've gotta talk." They proceeded to explain to me how, when you kiss or cuddle or hold hands with a boy, or even touch him at all, he can get "turned on." And if you "turn on" a boy but you don't intend to have sex with him because you're not married, then you're basically lying to him and telling his body that you can have sex even though you can't. "Defrauding" him, they called it. They explained that this isn't God's plan and that God wants all his followers to remain completely and totally "pure" until marriage and that girls should never "turn a boy on" (there was no discussion of whether girls could also be "turned on"). So in order to accomplish this, they said, the best plan was to never touch a boy whom you're dating. That's how you knew it was a good, godly relationship. Once you got engaged to be married, it was safe to hold hands, but you definitely couldn't kiss or do anything more than kiss until you got married.

I was a little confused. I didn't think kissing was a sin. I asked if it was, and they explained that even though it wasn't technically a sin, you couldn't do it without causing the boy to sin, so you had to treat it like a sin and stay far away. I closed my eyes and silently filed "kissing" away in my brain in the same category as "drinking alcohol." Not technically a sin, but so close to a sin that it might as well be a sin. OK.

At that moment, they produced a beautiful white-gold ring with an amethyst center stone—my birthstone. It was tucked inside a little black jewelry box and was the prettiest thing I'd ever seen. Purple was my favorite color. They said they wanted to give it to me as a symbol of my purity, but they could only give it to me if I absolutely promised not to hold hands with a boy until I was engaged to be married to him and not to kiss or have sex until after I was married.

If that was what it took to please God, I was down. If it pleased my parents at the same time? All the better. Hell, those two things were basically the same as far as I was concerned, and my parents never tried to untangle their dictates from God's. I wasn't sure how I felt about my sexual boundaries, but I figured it didn't matter how I felt because I had clearly been super wrong about the whole kissing thing. What did I know? I said yes. They gave me the ring. I put it on, and I proceeded to take my promise, and the strings attached to it, extremely seriously in the coming years.

And that was my sex education.

—

They say that you can boil a live frog in an open pot of water if you turn the heat up just a little bit at a time. This fact is usually used by preachers as a sermon illustration about the dangers of compromising your morals and sliding down the slippery slope, but the irony is that it's also a popular tactic abusive "men of God" use to ensnare their victims.

My own boiling began in high school.

My abuser operated under most people's radars at the aforementioned nondenominational evangelical mega-church my family attended. He was a quiet and unassuming man in his late twenties when I met him in the high school youth group when I was fourteen. A photographer and website designer by trade, he was extremely tech-savvy, so when he volunteered as a leader for the youth group, they put him to work operating PowerPoint presentations on the computer, taking pictures, and creating the youth group newsletter. A group of us students who were interested in technology coalesced around him, and he taught us the basics of Adobe suite products, photography, and other cool things we didn't have the opportunity to learn elsewhere.

He started singling me out early—paying me compliments, giving me more responsibilities than the other students, and even going so far as to pay me for doing nonchurch work for him, such as proofreading copy for websites he'd been contracted to build. Conversations slowly drifted from how to set up layers in InDesign to who I was dating, and I became accustomed, as many of the students did, to discussing the intimate details of my romantic life, what little there was, with him. He styled himself as a mentor and gave advice in a way that implied you'd be awfully foolish to do otherwise. In what I now recognize to be classic predatory grooming behavior, he even convinced me to break up with the person I was dating at fifteen. He told me it was because this boy wasn't godly enough, and if I really loved God, I wouldn't want to be with someone who didn't love God just as much.

At the start of my junior year of high school, I was single once again with my prized "kissginity" still intact. A new boy had come to our youth group that year and began trying to get me to go out with him—advances I initially dodged, but as time went on and he persisted, I began to wonder if maybe I shouldn't give him a shot. After all, he was so nice.

In October, I was sitting at a high-top table in the youth group room with my abuser, contemplating my next move, when I asked him, "What would you think if I dated Mark?" I remember his face twisting up, brow furrowing in what I interpreted in the moment to be genuine uncertainty but that was actually calculated, intentional, and planned well in advance. *Game.*

He blinked his eyes open and looked back up to make eye contact with me. The last moment before everything changed. *Set.*

"I'd be heartbroken." *Match.*

My world spun. My abuser was in his thirties by this time. I managed to quietly eke out, "You're old enough to be my father." Apparently not quietly enough; he shushed me.

I had to go home. I grabbed my younger brother from the other room and jumped in our family's fifteen-passenger van I'd driven there, gripping the cold plastic steering wheel with white knuckles the entire drive back to our house. Had he really said what I thought he'd said? Had he meant what I thought he'd meant by it? I got into bed as soon as I walked in the door and went to sleep, still trying to figure out if the whole night had been one weird fever dream.

—

In an ideal world, I would have immediately told my parents, my youth pastor, or another trusted adult what had happened. In an ideal world, I would have known that I needed to and the adults in my life would have known immediately that I was the victim of predatory behavior. But it was so confusing. My abuser *was* a trusted adult. My parents had him over for dinner regularly and knew and liked him. My dad had been my mom's youth pastor, after all—and my abuser hadn't kissed me or even tried to hold my hand, so it couldn't possibly be sinful! And anyway, I was sixteen years old. That was old enough for a romantic relationship with a man. Wasn't it?

I don't even know if I had heard the word *consent* spoken aloud ever, let alone knew what it meant or that it was negated by one party being a minor and the other party being a spiritual authority figure. Sex was as abstract to me then as kissing had been at thirteen. I didn't really know how it worked in practice or what my own body parts were called. I certainly didn't know that a romantic relationship between a teenage girl and an adult mentor in a religious setting was illegal in several states and unethical in all of them. I trusted him explicitly. He was a godly man who had my best interests at heart. He had told me that so many times.

—

I spent the next couple days stewing silently over what had happened. At that point, my abuser had normalized talking to me for hours every day even when we weren't at church. He always chatted with me through Gmail throughout the day, sending me messages to read later when I wasn't online.

But after that, there were no more chats, no more emails. Radio silence for days.

Finally, a few days later, an email arrived. Something about silence not being so golden. Something about how he was sorry if he offended me. Something about how he really thought it would be a God-honoring relationship.

A God-honoring relationship. *A God-honoring relationship?* I didn't know about that. But once I thought about it, I realized I had never known what honored God in a relationship. I thought it would be God-honoring to kiss after a few months of dating, but my parents told me that wasn't true. I thought my relationship with my boyfriend the year before had been God-honoring, but my abuser told me that it wasn't. Every time I thought I was on the right track, an authority figure had stepped in to show me that I wasn't pleasing God as much as I thought I was. And I really, really cared about pleasing God. More than I cared about anything. I couldn't stop thinking about how my mother was about my age when she started dating my father, and he had been in a position of spiritual authority over her too. Maybe *this* was finally the godly husband I had been promised. Maybe all those books I'd been given to read—*I Kissed Dating Goodbye* and *Boy Meets Girl* and all the others—maybe they were right! Maybe this was God's way of bringing me a spiritual leader who could tell me what was right and wrong and marry me as soon as I turned eighteen so that I wouldn't be tempted to sin by having sex outside of marriage. Maybe this was my ticket to holy sexuality, a way to bypass the death traps of "dating" and do what I was supposed to do as a woman: present myself as a pure and spotless bride to a deserving man of God.

—

When it comes to discussions about stress or trauma, most people are familiar with the concepts of "fight" and "flight." You either roundhouse kick the bear, or you run away from the bear. "Freeze" is another familiar one—like when a gazelle plays dead to avoid being chased by a lion. We humans share all of these physiological responses in common with the animal kingdom. But fewer people have heard of the fourth category of stress response, one unique to humans: "fawn." The fawn response happens when your subconscious believes that the best way for you to survive whatever is happening to you is to make nice with the source of the stress or trauma.

My friend Laura, who is a trauma therapist, puts it this way: fawn is "the nervous system response in which an individual may overly accommodate others in order to manage their fear. This may look like difficulty saying no or setting boundaries, anticipating the needs of others and lack of self-identity."[1]

I like the label "fawn" because it also describes what I was at sixteen. Young. Innocent. Naive. And very, very much in danger.

—

I saw my abuser the next week at youth group. I drove by him on the way out of the parking lot, and I pulled over and rolled my window down. "Hey!" I called out. "I think you might be right, what you said in the email." I remember the corners of his mouth turning up. I was his prey—his fawn—and I was staring down the barrel of his gun.

The following month consisted of stolen moments in dark corners of the church and closed offices and back seats of cars, daily emails and long chats spanning hours. He told me he loved me. He asked me what I wanted for a wedding present. He told me he couldn't wait until he could shower me with kisses. We had to keep it a secret, he said. Nobody would understand what we had; they would just misinterpret things. As the days went on, he was more aggressive, more graphic in his speech. Several weeks in, we returned to the church from running an errand with two other youth group members and lingered in the back seat of the car a few extra moments. The air was heavy with innuendo I couldn't possibly understand, and he leaned toward me, close enough that I could smell his cologne and feel his breath on my neck. "I don't want to go inside," he whispered. I felt the pit of my stomach drop twelve inches inside of me. I laughed it off, and we exited the car. The water was slowly coming to a rolling boil, building inexorably toward the moment when he would finally make a physical move.

Except by some miracle, that day never came.

One morning in November, my father asked my abuser to meet for coffee, and my abuser never emailed me again. I should have known it was coming, but optimistic as I was, I had hoped their meeting was just to talk about something church related. Later that afternoon, my parents cordoned me off in my bedroom and confronted me about my sin.

In what I can only describe as a tag-team decimation, they laid me and the situation bare. How could I do this? How could I think this was OK? It couldn't possibly be because of their history. Their story was different, they explained, because my father asked my mother's parents first. Obviously, that makes such a huge difference. I had lied to them and deceived them and entered into a "relationship" behind their backs. I was a liar and a sinner, and I brought this shame upon our family. I crumpled to the floor and sobbed. I shook and convulsed and curled into a ball. I had what

I later recognized to be a succession of panic attacks, one after the other, each new one arriving on the crest of a wave before the previous one had subsided. Eventually, I shut down. I completely dissociated from my body while they ranted and railed against me, their voices reverberating in my brain as if it were hollow. I felt like I was watching it happen from above. By the end of the conversation, I was catatonic, barely verbal, physically holding myself together with my own arms.

"We're going to give you one last phone call to him," they said. "To apologize." Their words didn't make any sense, but they handed me a phone and I took it. Unthinking, hyperfocused on my now singular goal of making this interaction end, I reflexively dialed his number. He picked up. I said his name. "I'm so sorry," he said. I told him I forgave him and mumbled some things I will never remember and that were probably inaudible through my sobs anyway. "I'm so sorry, I'm so sorry," I remember saying eventually. But he never said he forgave me. He never said anything. I said good-bye, and I waited and waited and waited, but there was only silence on the other end. I hung up the phone. Collapsed in a heap. After a few more minutes and promises that we weren't done talking about this, my parents finally left my room and shut my door behind them, leaving me utterly and completely alone.

—

At the age of twenty-seven, I was diagnosed with bipolar disorder after many years of chalking my extreme panic attacks up to bad anxiety. As with a lot of mental illnesses, doctors don't really know why exactly people develop bipolar. As best they can tell, you're born with a predisposition based on your gene pool, and a traumatic life event can trigger its development. My family history is rife with mental illness and substance abuse, so it's hard to say. What I do know is this. Later, when I looked back, I couldn't remember most of that winter. My parents continued to initiate interrogations with me for weeks after, convinced I wasn't telling them the whole truth about what had happened, driving me to panic attacks repeatedly and leaving me to pick the broken pieces of myself up off the bedroom floor over and over again when I could not produce the revelation they sought. They asked me repeatedly if he had kissed me, and if I thought he might be gay. Apparently only homosexuality could explain this kind of perversion. The conversations always ended with me in tears on the floor or running out the door to walk aimlessly around our neighborhood until my soul returned to my body. My relationship with my parents never recovered from the trauma of those early conversations.

My abuser was ousted from the youth group, the reasons quietly swept under the rug by church leadership too ignorant or cowardly or both to do the right thing. Gossip abounded. Some people knew; some people didn't. Lots of students who were loyal to my abuser but unaware of the reasons he was forced out were angry, and some even left the youth group over it. But life at the church went on, and I continued showing up each week, the shell of my body present in the chair but my mind and heart completely gone.

When the spring came and the fog began to lift, I was left with a big empty gap where my memories of time and events should have been. I had flashes of memory. I remembered the songs I would listen to as I walked around my neighborhood after my parents had another "conversation" with me. I remembered seeing the Trans-Siberian

Orchestra in concert at Christmastime, the way the high violin notes sent shivers up my spine and reminded me that I had a body. I remembered friends coming over to pick me up a lot, because part of my "punishment" for what I'd done was that my parents forbade me from driving anywhere but school. They also confiscated all my email and social media passwords and told me that I couldn't speak about what had happened to anyone but two close friends. As the months passed and I moved from the despair stage of grief to the bargaining stage, I began to handle my guilt over causing a church scandal and nearly destroying the youth group with my sinfulness by doubling down on my efforts at church. I was now there every Sunday, every Wednesday, every Saturday—sometimes twice a day. I was volunteering to watch babies and gardening for service projects and playing in the worship band and doing puppet shows for the kids and producing the youth group newsletter almost entirely by myself and generally running myself ragged hoping to atone for the wicked thing everyone told me I'd done. After a while, it started to feel like it was working.

And as the weather warmed, I began the slow ascent out of depression entirely. I planned three months' worth of internships, camps, and short-term mission trips, and I got the hell out of town for the summer. When I came back, I dated a nice boy my own age from youth group who knew the truth about what had happened to me the year before and didn't treat me like I was broken. We did normal high school things for a year, like going to prom and the movie theater. Still no kissing, but lots of healing. Eventually I applied to, and got into, Moody Bible Institute in Chicago, a fact that I wore like a first-place ribbon I won at the state fair in front of the adults in my life who had been looking at me like I was Jezebel in the flesh only a few months before.

The journey from evangelical bible college honors student to where I am now is one I will share in more detail throughout the rest of this book, but for now it is enough to say that in my early twenties, I began to deconstruct the purity teachings I had been handed down as gospel. I also learned about consent, which showed me more clearly that what had happened to me when I was sixteen wasn't my fault. Over time, my feelings shifted from lingering guilt and uncertainty to outright anger. The more I learned, the more I realized how shameful and ludicrous it was that not a single adult in my life at the time realized that a relationship between a sixteen-year-old with no sex education and a man in his thirties who was supposed to be a spiritual authority figure at church could not possibly be consensual. And yet it had been treated like a coequal perpetration of sin and not the predatory campaign of manipulation and grooming that it was.

Attempting to look at the situation objectively, I could see that there were many reasons for the trauma I endured, ranging from ignorance, to cowardice, to bad hermeneutics, to outright deception and evil. But the fact remains that literally every person and system in place that should have protected me as a child failed me—from my family, to my church, to individual adults who should have known better. They failed me thoroughly and spectacularly. The fact that a sixteen-year-old who had been groomed for abuse by a male church leader in his thirties would ever be made to call him and *apologize* and then be punished for it is a testament to the gruesomely backward moral system that undergirds the theology of sexuality in the conservative evangelical church.

—

I had told the world. *Now what?* I was almost afraid to look. I wanted to shut my laptop and perhaps buy a nice piece of property in Montana and go off the grid, never to be heard from on a website called "Twitter" again. But I managed to hit refresh, and I realized in the intervening minutes that I had been getting responses from people. Lots of responses. Several women reached out to tell me that something similar had happened to them. A woman I'd known for a decade who was also abused by my abuser took the opportunity to come forward publicly too.

My phone buzzed. My friend River, who had been in the group text I sent, wrote, "People obviously want to talk about this. I think we need to find some kind of way to compile these stories."

River and I had been running blogs together since college, so I agreed. "People are clearly hungry for it, and I think it deserves its own conversation," I texted back. "What about a hashtag?"

We batted a few ideas back and forth. "How about #ChurchToo? It's short like #MeToo and people will get it," I texted River.

"OK, #ChurchToo," they said.

"Great, you tweet it out and I'm going to bed," I replied, knowing I probably wouldn't get much sleep but also knowing I should try, since I was leaving on a trip out of town early the next morning. River sent a tweet letting people know that #ChurchToo was the tag to use if they wanted to continue the conversation, and I went to bed. I expected our collectively modest Twitter following to engage with the tag, and I figured we'd probably have a few dozen stories to share and amplify.

What I didn't expect was to wake up to thousands of tweets and counting. But that's what happened. And that is what has been happening every day since.

Throughout the weekend that followed, I was glued to my phone. The whole thing felt so tender and in need of careful formation and guidance, and I became very protective of the conversation. As the hashtag and the stories came into the spotlight and began showing up on major media websites, so did the immediate criticism. Within the first twenty-four hours, people were accusing us of being "angry feminists" (true), "atheists who just want to destroy the church" (false), and "lesbians with an agenda" (I guess technically half true, though I wouldn't come out as gay for another year after #ChurchToo launched). There were also a lot of don't-throw-the-baby-out-with-the-bathwater-isms from well-meaning religious folk concerned that the exposure of the rot of sexual abuse in their communities would put people off from going to church altogether.

And then some people glommed onto the tag like remora fish as soon as they saw how popular it was and tried to use it to promote their own messages that undercut the true meaning of #ChurchToo, claiming that the church had obviously messed up when it came to talking and teaching about sex but that it was still vitally important to be heterosexual and abstinent until marriage. Many of them claimed that men were still God's ordained leaders; they just needed to do a better job of properly reporting instances of sexual abuse that occurred under their leadership. I also saw that if we weren't careful, the campaign would be turned into a "women's issue" that had nothing to do with the way the church taught about sexuality at all. I wanted no part in that watered-down message, and I took great pains to guide the conversation as closely as I could in those first few days, as I knew that's when it would be most vulnerable to misinterpretation.

In the days, weeks, and months that followed, River and I practically did interviews as a part-time job. There were so many we often had to divide them up just to get through our week. Our stories were featured on *Time*, the Huffington Post, Jezebel, *Mother Jones*, the *New Yorker*, Bustle, *Teen Vogue*, and dozens of other magazines and websites. We took interviews from other countries—Colombia, Australia, France. We did podcasts, recorded videos, took speaking gigs, wrote our own articles. I appeared on CNN's *United Shades of America* with comedian W. Kamau Bell and told my story on national television. *Cosmopolitan* even sent a photographer to take pictures of me for the print edition of the magazine. It seemed everybody who heard about it was desperate to dig deeper into the problem of sexual abuse in faith communities.

And as the movement continued to gain traction and big names in evangelical Christianity started seeing even a handful of consequences for their actions—some of whose stories I will explore later in this book—one of the most common questions asked of me personally and also shouted out into the void of the internet was "What can we do?" Pastors, lay leaders, congregants, survivors, and even those who no longer attended church all wanted to know what, if anything, could be done to start to stem the tide of these abuses that now seemed so ubiquitous. Their queries filled up my inboxes and DMs and continue to do so even now.

And I am sorry to report that if you came to this book looking for a list of things you can do to absolve your church community from responsibility for this problem, you have come to the wrong place. If you're a pastor or a youth pastor or a parent of teenagers, you are just going to have to sit in your discomfort for a while as you work through this material. This book is not a Here's-How-to-Be-a-Less-Problematic-Church manual, and while I suggest a number of potential action steps throughout the book, they are all costly. The answers are not simple, or fun, and they will not allow the existing power structures to be maintained. They require radical deconstruction of closely held beliefs and the willingness to sacrifice personal gain and social goodwill to do the right thing. And if that cannot be accomplished, they require the bravery to leave and do the right thing elsewhere.

I think often of the biblical story of Jesus and the rich young ruler, found in the gospels of Mark and Matthew (Mark 10 and Matthew 19, respectively). The rich young ruler comes to Jesus and, like many religious people and communities today, asks, "What can I do?" Jesus tells him that though he has kept the commandments, he also must sell everything and follow him. And then the rich young ruler goes away sad because he cannot do the thing that actually costs him.

My hope is that we are all brave enough to do that which costs us.

Survivors, this book is written for you, by you, and with you in mind. I will pull no punches fighting for justice for you, for myself, for all of us, whatever that looks like. Thank you for trusting me enough to follow along with me on this journey.

For pastors, church leaders, and others still deeply embedded in the American Christian industrial complex who are for whatever reason reading this book—buckle up.

1

KEEP YOUR WAY PURE...OR ELSE

How can young people keep their way pure?
By guarding it according to your word.

—Psalm 119:9

My father was an English teacher for part of my childhood. I inherited my love of writing from him, and he taught my siblings and me innumerable lessons about language and communication. One thing he used to say—that I still often repeat when I teach writing workshops—is this: "Specific is terrific." If you're going to have a good conversation, you can't speak in vague abstractions. You have to define your terms.

Anyone who has ever been on the receiving end of a Christian friend or relative "speaking the truth in love" knows that Christians across the board have vastly different definitions for words like *love*, *truth*, *Jesus*, and more, even if they are technically using the same words when they speak. But in order to understand the dynamics of the abuse that takes place in Christian churches, families, and communities, it is necessary to have a handle on the words, concepts, and histories at play. I won't be attempting to demonstrate that abuse occurs ubiquitously in these environments for the same reason I won't be attempting to prove that the sky is blue. What I will be attempting to do, however, is demonstrate *how* the very specific theological and cultural aspects of many of our churches, schools, and other ministries both enable abusers and retraumatize survivors. Because as we know, abuse occurs everywhere. While it is a Christian problem, it is also a problem in other religions, and among the nonreligious, and in Washington and Hollywood, and across all political party lines. So why call out #ChurchToo specifically?

As much as many evangelical Christians may like to claim otherwise, the most popular modern Christian teaching on human sexuality in the West—that the only right expression of sexuality is between a man and a woman in a lifelong, monogamous, legal marriage—is not and has never been "the historic Christian position" on the topic. Leaving aside the fact that state-sanctioned marriage for the sake of romantic love is a historically recent invention and not a category any writer of the bible would have been familiar with, the biblical writers themselves have very little to say on the topic—outside of a few scattered verses throughout the biblical canon, the significance of which hinge on the translation of several Greek and Hebrew words whose true meanings are uncertain and hotly debated.

Now, before you check out on me, don't worry. After this paragraph, I will dedicate exactly zero words of this book to pointing out why such-and-such verse doesn't actually say the thing conservative Christians say it does. After many years of having these conversations, I've come to realize that we can bible-bomb each other back and forth all day long, but if someone is bound and determined to translate *porneia* as "fornication," there is no hermeneutical appeal you can possibly make to stop them. Translating *porneia* as "fornication" is not a hermeneutical decision but rather an ideological one. Not only that, but regardless of "what the text actually says," I am more interested in the question of *how it is used*. And while I'll list several of my favorite resources for sex-positive Christian theology and engaging with many of the "clobber verses" (as they are so often called) concerning human sexuality in the appendix in the back of the book, doing sex-positive theology is not my project here, for three reasons.

First, other people have already done that work better than I could: liberation theologians and womanists and people with more advanced degrees from schools where you couldn't also get academic credit for praying in front of the Planned Parenthood down the street. Second, a sex-positive Christian theology is not the most useful path forward for everyone (more on this at the end of the book). And third, as a friend of mine posted on Facebook the other day, "Not all problematic sacred passages are misinterpreted."[1] I think it's up to each individual to decide what their relationship with the bible will be, but I do not advocate an approach that requires that everything in the bible be "without error" or shoehorned into a meaning that doesn't offend people with twenty-first-century understandings of things like human sexuality, consent, or social justice.

But without attempting to reinterpret every bible verse that even remotely refers to human sexuality, I must point out that the necessity of abstinence until heterosexual marriage simply did not seem to be a huge concern at the time the bible was written. I'm not at all claiming that Christianity has always had a historically positive view of sex and the body—but I suspect even Paul would be a little flabbergasted by most True Love Waits talking points.

But here's the thing: lying about something having always been a particular way is one of the ways that abusive power structures are maintained. Many people in Christian churches today are terrified to question the doctrines of sexuality they are being told are "orthodoxy" by their pastors and leaders because they feel like they would be questioning God themself and not an invention of the late twentieth century born out of white supremacy and anxiety about the sexual revolution.

But I'm getting ahead of myself. First we need to talk a little history.

A Short History of Everything . . . Purity

If we were all at my kitchen table right now, I'd pour you each a big glass of wine to get through this part because there are a lot of dates and resolutions and amendments, but I promise if you read to the end, you'll have a much better understanding of *why* we're in the situation we're currently in when it comes to #ChurchToo.

The modern "purity" movement as we know it today only came about in the last few decades as a result of political forces much larger than itself. Much has been written about the galvanization of evangelicals around the issue of resisting desegregation *years* before being antiabortion became a litmus test of true Christianity, and if you ever have a spare afternoon, I highly recommend falling down that particular Google rabbit hole. But for our purposes here, I think it is important to point out that up until the mid-to-late 1970s, issues related to human sexuality were not a primary aspect of political activism and social organizing for evangelical Christians. Evangelical leaders and politicians were far more preoccupied with protecting "religious liberty" as the government began to rescind the tax-exempt status of private (read whites-only) schools that had formed in response to the desegregation mandate.[2] In fact, when it came to the issue of abortion, in 1971 the Southern Baptist Convention passed a resolution supporting "legislation that will allow the possibility of abortion under such conditions as rape, incest, clear evidence of severe fetal deformity, and carefully ascertained evidence of the likelihood of damage to the emotional, mental, and physical health of the mother," and they reaffirmed that position in 1974 and 1976 (*Roe v. Wade* was ruled on in 1973).[3] Evangelicals by and large had little interest in getting into the weeds about abortion because at the time it was considered a Catholic issue.

But that all changed when it became clear that continuing to resist desegregation was futile and also made evangelicals look like The Bad Guys™. So over the course of a few short years between 1970 and 1980, the dialogue shifted from desegregation to abortion because, as Fred Clark on his blog *Slacktivist* notes, "redefine abortion as baby-killing and you redefine everyone who supports it as a baby-killer. And you're always guaranteed to hold the moral high-ground."[4] In that same blog, Clark says of the belief that life begins at conception and that Christianity is essentially pro-life that "no white evangelical born before 1970 grew up believing this. No white evangelical born after 1980 grew up not believing this."[5]

So why all the talk about abortion? Isn't this supposed to be about purity?

Stick with me. I contend that the brand-new evangelical Christian obsession with abortion in the late 1970s and early 1980s as a result of losses in the battle against desegregation is intimately connected to the birth of the modern purity movement. At its heart, abortion is a question of sexual control. Who will reproduce? Does it matter if they want to or not? And along with abortion come other issues: contraception, sexual orientation, marriage, and more. The antiabortion movement among evangelical Christians in my lifetime has consistently been skeptical of contraception (at best), exclusive of nonheterosexual sexual identities, and focused on the preservation of the institution of marriage to the detriment of the health and well-being of the actual human beings inside the institution.

This theory starts to make a little more sense when you note that True Love Waits, the prototypical evangelical abstinence-only "sex ed" program, has its roots in a "Christian Sex Education project" begun by cofounder Jimmy Hester in 1987.[6] By 1992, True Love Waits was a part of LifeWay, and by 1994, they had stuck 102,000 abstinence pledge cards from young people on the lawn of the Orlando Convention Center during the Southern Baptist Convention. The book *Why Wait?* by Joshua McDowell came out that same year, and *I Kissed Dating Goodbye* by Joshua Harris, who has since renounced some of the views he espoused in that book and deconverted from Christianity entirely, followed in 1997.

Also happening during this time? The AIDS crisis.

The mid-to-late 1970s was a time of increasing evangelical organization around not just abortion but homosexuality. Tim LaHaye's book *The Unhappy Gays* (the same Tim LaHaye who would later coauthor the hit apocalyptic Left Behind series with Jerry B. Jenkins, who had a parking spot outside my dorm building at Moody), which portrayed LGBTQ persons as mentally ill deviants who would rather be sick and alienated from their families and society than submit to the will of God, was released in 1978—the same year that Christians were attempting to pass Proposition 6 in the state of California, which would have allowed public schools to fire gay and lesbian teachers on the basis of their sexuality. The AIDS crisis is considered to have started in 1981, and by 1987, when the crisis was well underway, Senator Jesse Helms of North Carolina attached an amendment to a spending bill "designed to prevent the federal government from paying for any AIDS education or prevention materials that would 'promote or encourage, directly or indirectly, homosexual sexual activities.'"[7]

In spite of the suffering the gay community was experiencing, many Christians were calloused toward the AIDS crisis and even viewed it as a just punishment for those aforementioned "homosexual sexual activities." Jerry Falwell Sr. of Liberty University, one of the largest Christian universities in the world, famously stated during the crisis that "AIDS is not just God's punishment for homosexuals, it is God's punishment for the society that tolerates homosexuals."[8] Helms's amendment certainly seemed to view it that way: "The CDC immediately adopted strict guidelines that applied to every pamphlet, flier, and poster it printed or paid for. The agency said 'no,' for example, to any picture of the genital organs, the anus, and either safe *or* unsafe sex. In addition, all prevention materials had to warn about the dangers of promiscuity and IV drug use and propound the benefits of abstinence."[9]

Oh yeah, and speaking of abstinence, the Adolescent Family Life Act (AFLA), emphasizing abstinence until marriage, was first passed in 1981, the same year the AIDS crisis started. They called it "the chastity act" at the time.[10] By 1996, there was a whole eight-point system of what constituted "abstinence-only education" according to the government, including topics like the expectation of monogamy in marriage, the potential of drug and alcohol use to put young people at risk of sexual advances, and the dangers of out-of-wedlock pregnancy and sexually transmitted infections (STIs).[11] The fight over abstinence-only versus medically accurate and consent-based sex education in schools continues to this day, and we will look at it more in chapter 5.

And one more thing. From the mid-1980s to the mid-1990s, violence against abortion clinics and abortion providers increased exponentially. Kidnappings, assaults, shootings, and bombings were regular features in the news, and many of the perpetrators of this violence identified as devout Christians who were doing what they felt God called them to do.

OK. Whew. Take a breath. History lesson over.

So what's the moral of the story?

Far from being an essential feature of historic Christianity, the popular purity teachings of today are a result of white anxiety around being able to produce enough well-behaved Christian babies to remain in charge of Western society. This relatively recent soup we're all swimming in is the basis of the modern purity movement—or what many people refer to as *purity culture.* You may have heard that term before, and you may have noticed that I haven't used it in this book yet, for a very specific reason.

Back in my day, many years ago, when Twitter was just a vast wasteland flowing with primordial ooze and there was no Donald Trump and you could tweet at restaurants and get free coupons any time you wanted and the spirit of God was hovering over the waters, *purity culture* arose as a term to describe what many people were beginning to write about then—this system of sexual *dos* and *don'ts* that had been passed down to Christians of an entire generation as gospel truth. Authors Donna Freitas and Jessica Valenti both used the term in books during that time, and it became popular on the internet as a phrase that signified both the religious corollary of rape culture (the societal injustices that enable and excuse assault and abuse) and the theological teachings that uphold that culture.[12] For many years, those of us who were doing work at the intersection of faith and sexuality used the phrase *purity culture* easily and seamlessly, and whenever we used it, people knew that we were talking about the culture created by theologies like male leadership, modesty, abstinence-only sex education, and other doctrines that allowed abuse and dysfunction to thrive.

But as with all popular and useful phrases, *purity culture* has recently fallen prey to the phenomenon of concept creep. Just as *emotional labor* has come to be used to mean "helping my friends with their problems" or "remembering my relatives' birthdays,"[13] *purity culture* is now often used by evangelical Christians still deeply committed to teaching its doctrines to refer to the more obvious, extreme examples of abstinence-only teachings—such as metaphors wherein nonvirgins are compared to chewed-up gum or Harris's flat prohibition of all dating relationships in *I Kissed Dating Goodbye*. These teachings, we are assured by these evangelical Christians, got the grace of God wrong. They focused too much on a list of things not to do and not enough on Jesus. Sexual sin like having sex before marriage or giving in to your same-sex desires isn't any worse than any other sin, you see! And, according to them, the answer isn't to throw the purity baby out with purity culture bathwater—the answer is, as Joe Carter recently stated

in an article for the neo-Calvinist evangelical website the
Gospel Coalition, to "develop a positive culture of purity."[14]
In other words, they believe the problem isn't the message;
it's the method.

(It's worth noting that I'm blocked by the Gospel Coalition on Twitter because several years ago, when a sexual
abuse scandal was uncovered in several of their member
churches, the hashtag #IStandWithSGMVictims—SGM for
Sovereign Grace Ministries—started trending on Twitter,
and the administrators of the Gospel Coalition's account
went through the tag systematically blocking everyone who
was using it in a supportive light. Positive culture of purity,
indeed!)

But that's not what *purity culture* means. *Purity culture*
refers to the culture created *by the specific doctrines* about
human sexuality that are taught in conservative Christian
environments. It *can* include the chewed-gum metaphors
and the abstinence "educators" screaming in your face about
STIs . . . or it might be the kind, hip small group leader
teaching the high school girls that God is gracious and for-
giving, but it's still important to stay pure until marriage to
your prince charming. The delivery method isn't nearly as
crucial to the definition as the content of the message.

Reducing purity culture to Christians just being "mean" or
"extreme" about certain theologies belies the very real harm
done by those theologies themselves and allows people to
benefit from looking like they are allies in the fight against
abuse while simultaneously upholding the beliefs that create
the culture of abuse in the first place. Sometimes people want
to uphold those beliefs because they are scared. Sometimes
people want to uphold those beliefs because they truly don't
understand the interpretive and hermeneutical issues at
play. And sometimes people want to uphold those beliefs

because they have vested financial interests in the resources afforded to them by performing the beliefs publicly—jobs in conservative churches, book deals with conservative publishers, social connections with other people who perform those beliefs, and so on. Think of what has happened to people in the public sphere like singer and musician Jennifer Knapp or writer Jen Hatmaker or even purity culture darling Joshua Harris when they announced that they were separating themselves from a strict, conservative Christian sexual ethic. They were crucified. And when public figures are crucified in this way, the regular people in the pews get the unequivocal message that if they step out of line, this is what's going to happen to them too. Not exactly a context for good moral reasoning, in my opinion.

Defining Purity Culture

Ask anybody who works at the intersection of faith and sexuality what purity culture is and you will probably get a slightly different answer from each person. I've been working on my elevator pitch for quite a few years now, and it's still pretty wordy, but so am I:

> Purity culture is the spiritual corollary of rape culture created in Christian environments by theologies that teach complete sexual abstinence until legal, monogamous marriage between a cisgender, heterosexual man and a cisgender, heterosexual woman for life— or else.

I know that's a lot, so let's go over it piece by piece.

We've already talked about purity culture being the spiritual corollary of rape culture. It's basically TyraBanks.gif,

"Rape culture, but make it Jesus." (For my older readers, this is a reference to a scene from the reality TV show *America's Next Top Model,* a show I have never watched because I was homeschooled.) But what about the rest?

- *Complete sexual abstinence.* Different families, denominations, and communities will vary on how far they take this. My own family of origin was on the extreme side of the spectrum by asking me not to even *hold hands* with someone until I had already become engaged to marry them. Other communities are fine with holding hands and kissing, but any kind of nonmarital sexual contact is still off-limits. Still other Christians will consider themselves "virgins" (a term that has no medical or scientific definition) as long as they have not had penetrative intercourse that involves a penis and a vagina.
- *Legal, monogamous marriage.* It's not enough to be deeply in love with or committed to someone, or be intending to marry them, or be partnered with them for many years. For most Christians who teach purity culture, there has to be some kind of legal paperwork or ceremony in order for the marriage to "count" and for any subsequent sexual activity not to be sin. Also, this probably goes without saying, but the marriage must be monogamous. Any concept of nonmonogamy or polyamory is anathema, and no distinction is made between ethical nonmonogamy and adultery or cheating.
- *Between a cisgender heterosexual man and a cisgender heterosexual woman. Cisgender* means that you identify with the gender identity the adults around you ascribed to you when you were born. There really

isn't any room in purity culture for transgender, nonbinary, or intersex folks. And nonheterosexual sexual orientations are ignored at best and actively demonized at worst. Often those who identify as gay, lesbian, or bisexual are expected to "surrender their sexuality" to God and either remain single and celibate or marry someone their community would consider the "opposite sex." Many are even forced into conversion therapy, where they attempt to "change" their sexuality through prayer or other "treatments." The purity culture ideal for relationships is a straight man with a penis and a straight woman with a vagina, and that's all.

- *For life.* Divorce is highly stigmatized. The expectation is usually that unless you prove egregious wrongdoing on the part of the other person, you are obligated to stay in your marriage for life. Often, even when wrongdoing is uncovered, the wronged party is encouraged or expected to forgive their partner, and the couple is expected to move on together. Prolonging the marriage is always viewed as the best choice, even when it leads to poor mental health outcomes for the adults or the children.

- *Or else.* What exactly constitutes "or else" varies, again, among families, denominations, and communities. The threat hanging over my head growing up was that God would be mad at me and, secondarily, that if I failed to live up to the purity ideal, I would someday have to explain my failure to a potential future spouse, and he (always he) would have to think long and hard about it and decide if he still wanted me. Other communities tell young people that if they have sex outside of marriage, they'll

almost certainly get pregnant or contract any number of STIs because condoms don't work, and people
who stray from God's plan deserve these things. Still
others use parental dissatisfaction, social rejection,
dissatisfying future marriages, and even the threat of
burning in hell forever to enforce this sexual ethic.

Purity culture is the culture in our churches, schools, families, and parachurch ministries *created by these theologies*. It
doesn't have anything to do with the delivery method or
what metaphors you use or how nicely you say it. If, at the
end of the day, someone is still teaching that complete sexual abstinence until legal, monogamous marriage between a
cisgender, heterosexual man and a cisgender, heterosexual
woman for life is a universal moral obligation, or else, then
guess what? They're still teaching purity culture.

How Does Purity Culture Uphold a Culture of Abuse?

Imagine a community with tons of eager, well-meaning
young people who really want to please God. Imagine that
this group of young people has little to no sex education
and may not even know words like *consent* or the accurate
names for their own body parts. Imagine that sex is viewed
simultaneously as the trophy at the end of the race toward
which they strive and the monster hiding in the closet that
could destroy them without warning. Now further imagine
that the young women in this group have been told that
they are the gatekeepers of the young men's sexual purity.
Imagine that they have been told that it's their job to dress
modestly and enforce sexual boundaries because men
are "visual creatures" and can't help getting turned on by

beauty. Imagine that they've also been told that men are the God-ordained leaders in relationships and that good women practice submission. Imagine that they've been told this is all required according to the way the people in power interpret a sacred book, and if they don't fall in line, they are putting themselves at risk.

And now imagine that all of this takes place in a community where those people in power are very concerned about looking good to outsiders. Imagine that some of those in power are more committed to being in power than to doing the right thing. Imagine that they have little understanding of the difference between a sin and a crime, and imagine that a violation of the sexual ethic they hold so dear is the worst thing they can think of. Imagine that they have made their communal purity the hallmark of their identity. Imagine that they have so much internalized shame around sex that they are determined that everyone else should be shameful about it as well and just keep their mouths shut so that we don't make someone uncomfortable or ruin someone's life. And imagine that they publicly laud the virtues of love, forgiveness, and second chances as central to what it means to be a member of their faith.

Now, not to put too fine a point on it, but is this not a giant, flashing "WELCOME" sign to predators, abusers, narcissists, and people with ulterior motives of all kinds? I'm picturing one of those light-up arrows outside a motel reading "VACANCY," except instead it says, "You Will Definitely Be Able to Find Your Next Victim Here, and We Probably Won't Even Press Charges!" Sadly, most of us know that this thought experiment is anything but hypothetical. Many of the churches and religious communities we grew up being a part of represented some if not all of the factors I mentioned and still others that I didn't. And those of us who are survivors know intimately just how toxic this kind of environment can be.

But it's the shame that I mentioned above that is key here. Purity culture is a direct path to sexual shame. Different people respond differently to purity culture, and often our privilege insulates us from consequences that people with less privilege have no choice but to internalize. So not everyone will be carrying ten tons of baggage with them into adulthood. But almost everyone who grew up in purity culture exhibits signs or attitudes of sexual shame. And sexual shame is one of the main things that leads churches into silence when someone is abused in their midst.

Sexual Shame

Purity culture can also be thought of as a culture of *sexual shame*. At its core, shame alienates us from ourselves and from others. What exactly shame is and how we work with it has been the topic of dozens of other books. Researcher Brené Brown popularized a now oft-used definition distinguishing shame and guilt in which guilt is an awareness that we *did* something bad and shame is a belief that we *are* bad.[15] In his book *Beyond Shame*, author and licensed therapist Matthias Roberts says, "Shamefulness is based on the presupposition that there is a 'right' context for sexual expression and a 'wrong' context for it"[16] and that "it is what lurks behind so many scandals and so much harm that gets swept under the rug to maintain and preserve images."[17] In other words, as author Linda Kay Klein points out, "The purity message is not about sex. Rather, it's about *us*: who we are, who we are expected to be, and who it is said we will become if we fail to meet those expectations. This is the language of shame."[18]

Very few churches, even those that self-identify as "progressive," have a healthy, open dialogue in their community about sex and sexuality. I myself remember being shamed by my parents growing up for asking questions or bringing up sexual topics (which I learned quickly not to do anymore), and the "dialogue" at my church was limited to separating the boys from the girls one Wednesday night each February so that the boys could go to one room and talk about pornography and the girls could go to another room and talk about boys. This shoved any real dialogue about sex underground, and we were left to get much-needed information from the internet, outdated library books, and other teens in hushed conversations. We certainly knew we couldn't talk to the adults in our lives, because they would only parrot back to us the single set of beliefs we were each expected to hold.

One of the most common questions I get when I speak and give interviews is "OK, so how exactly does shame lead to abuse?" And this is how: shame alienates us from ourselves and our own internal compass and sense of what we do and don't want. It also alienates us from others. It *isolates* us, which is a primary pillar of abuse. It makes us afraid to talk to others because we are afraid we will be punished for having experiences that are outside the boundaries of their expectations. Often, as was the case with me and my story, we *actually are punished,* so this fear is validated and reinforced. Shame also makes it difficult for the people who uncover the abuse, because if they are inundated with purity culture, they are likely just as misinformed or ignorant about healthy sexuality as the victim, and they are terrified of giving the church a bad name and letting the world know that this sexual purity thing they've used to unflinchingly define the boundaries of their community doesn't work. Shame turns the lights off in the room, and abuse thrives where there are secrecy and cover.

Not only does shame make abuse that has already occurred worse, but I would go so far as to say that the sexual shame that comes from purity culture actually sets the stage for abuse to be *more* widespread than it otherwise would be in churches and other Christian environments. I don't mean that sexual shame makes abuse happen in a causal manner—there are lots of people carrying lots of sexual shame who have never abused anyone, and abuse happens because people with agency and autonomy choose to abuse. As my friend Laura said on a podcast recently, "Abuse is not a behavior; it's a value system."[19]

But we can walk and chew gum at the same time, and we can also acknowledge that people who have a value system that includes abusing others are overwhelmingly attracted to places like evangelical Christian churches, where purity culture is the normative sexual ethic. We can acknowledge that when you raise young men in this environment from a young age, it is going to be damn near impossible for them to emerge with a value system that views women and vulnerable people as fully loved, fully equal humans who deserve to have a say in what happens to their bodies and who deserve to say yes or no to the type of sex they want to have and when and with whom they want to have it. We can acknowledge that when you try to force all sexuality other than one particular expression into a suitcase, sit on top of it, and try to zip it shut even if it doesn't fit, that suitcase is going to break eventually, and then you'll have more problems than you did before.

We can look at the role culture plays in abuse while also holding abusers ultimately and finally accountable for their actions. Abuse is *always* the fault of the abuser, and the culture of a church will either reward or punish abusive behavior—attract it or repel it. Purity culture is fundamentally complicit in abuse.

It's also worth noting that many abusers in Christian communities are behaving in ways that are perfectly in line with the theological beliefs their communities hold about sex, gender, and sexuality. Rather than misinterpreting or making theological missteps, Christian abusers are often taking what they are taught in the pulpit (or what they are teaching from the pulpit) and putting it into practice in their lives.

Now wait just a second, Emily—are you saying that there are Christian denominations out there that teach that sexual assault is right and holy? Obviously not. Not like that, anyway. But there are lots of Christian denominations out there that teach theologies whose logical outcome is sexual dysfunction and sexual abuse. It's like setting a house on fire and convening a conference to talk about the ashes. We need to confiscate the matches.

—

As you move through the rest of this book, you'll be confronted with stories—my own and others'—and the ways that the various doctrines of purity culture move in and through these stories to create the foundation on which these traumatizing experiences are built. I will also describe the uniquely retraumatizing events that often occur after abuse in Christian churches, families, and communities. I'll explore these theologies in detail and suggest ways to counteract their effects in your life and the lives of those around you.

And I do start from the assumption that they should be counteracted. Those who have ears to hear will hear, and those who don't won't, but if you are committed to upholding the theologies of purity culture but looking for a way you can do so without contributing to the problem of #ChurchToo, you have come to the wrong place. I believe the Southern Baptist Convention is working on that right now, but they might be a little busy dealing with the hundreds of recently revealed cases of alleged sexual assault by pastors in their denomination.[20]

A generation of people who were raised in the purity culture that arose out of the 1970s, 1980s, and 1990s in North America are now reckoning with the consequences of those theologies on their lives. Some have found solace in a different kind of Christianity, whereas others have discovered alternative religious practices or left religion entirely. Many have experienced broken relationships with others and with themselves, and many have sought therapy and psychiatric care to help manage the ongoing consequences. Yes, not all people who grew up in this very specific, historically recent purity culture were negatively affected. But enough people were that those who continue to turn away from the problem because they are not willing to do the work of unlearning purity culture can only be considered calloused toward the plight of countless survivors. We are only beginning to uncover the damage that was done. #ChurchToo is a part of that. It is an unveiling of that which has existed all along.

And for the rest of this book, I'm going to show you why.

2

FOR WOMEN WHO PROFESS REVERENCE FOR GOD

I desire, then, that in every place the men should pray, lifting up holy
hands without anger or argument; also that the women should dress
themselves modestly and decently in suitable clothing . . . with good
works, as is proper for women who profess reverence for God.

—1 Timothy 2:8–10

In June 2019, the Southern Baptist Convention (SBC)
released a fifty-two-page report on sexual abuse in their
own denomination in anticipation of their annual gathering in Birmingham, Alabama, that same month. The report
claimed, among other things, that a key reason there was
so much sexual abuse in their ranks was because of something it referred to as "theological misapplications."[1] In
other words, the theology itself was not the problem but

merely the misapplication of it by sinful people. "Theological misapplications"—what a turn of phrase. In two words, the SBC shifted the blame off of their own shoulders and onto those who were criticizing them. Can't their critics see—if we could stop being so biased and emotional for just a moment—that it's merely a few bad actors who have taken good theology and applied it inappropriately? The theology itself could never be at fault—that would be heresy.

And while this entire book is predicated on the assertion that, contra the SBC's report, there is no such thing as "theological misapplication"—good theology bears good fruit, bad theology bears bad fruit, especially when it comes to purity culture and abuse—I think it's especially apparent when it comes to this first theological teaching I'll be exploring: modesty.

—

Every man is staring at you. When you wear those tight little shorts, every man is staring at your butt. When you wear the tight, revealing shirt, every guy is looking at your breasts. Think about that the next time you get dressed. Think about your grandfather, because all of his old friends are looking at your breasts when you wear that stuff. Eww! I know it's gross, but that's the truth. If you dress like a piece of meat, you're gonna get thrown on the BBQ. It's that simple.

—Justin Lookadoo[2] and Hayley Morgan, *Dateable*[3]

The idea that Christians need to be "modest" comes from a few different verses in the bible, but 1 Timothy 9 (which I quoted at the start of this chapter) is specifically weaponized by evangelical Christians against women and young girls to control what they wear. Because of the way this verse is popularly interpreted, the importance of modesty, pretty much exclusively for women, is a near universal in purity culture. What's less universal, however, is the definition of what exactly constitutes "modest."

Growing up, "modesty" was defined in my house according to the latest book my mother had read. One summer, it would be OK for us girls to wear tank tops outside. The next summer—no tank tops, only T-shirts. The summer after that, tank tops were OK again as long as we wore two at a time to make the straps appear wider and cover the oh-so-scandalous errant bra strap. Some conservative Christian communities take it as far as mandating that women only wear skirts in public, whereas communities more to the center of the spectrum tend to grapple with questions like whether yoga pants or bikinis are acceptable for women to wear. In addition, you'll notice vastly different communal understandings of what it means to be "modest" in a church in the desert of Arizona in July, for example, versus a church in central Illinois.

But regardless of *how* a community defines modesty, the moral imperative for women to dress a certain way in order to avoid leading the men in the community into sinful behavior is ubiquitous. Almost without fail, the reasoning given for modest dressing is as follows: When you show too much skin, men, who are "visual creatures," can't help but start thinking sexual thoughts about you and may even become physically aroused. It's in their God-given nature to do this, because they're visually stimulated in a way that women aren't. Once you've been made aware of this as a woman, if you continue to dress in a way that provokes sexual thoughts in men, you are morally culpable and part of the problem, since men should only be thinking sexual thoughts about their wives.

Now, it's a *very* small hop, skip, and a jump from this line of reasoning to blaming a woman for her own assault because of what she was wearing (or not wearing) when it occurred. The quote from *Dateable* that I opened this section with makes that exquisitely clear. But that's why I chose it, right? Because it perfectly illustrates my point? Surely I just picked the worst quote I could find to make conservative Christians look bad for trying to help women value themselves and resist our sex-saturated culture, as they say.

I wish I was being histrionic. Head over to Twitter and spend a few minutes perusing the #ChurchToo hashtag. You'll find plenty of stories of women who, upon reporting their assault at the hands of a pastor or youth pastor, were asked, "Well, what were you wearing?" The barbecue quote is an extreme example, sure. But without using the same language, modesty teachings are telling Christian women every day that they're in danger of being thrown on the barbecue if they don't dress exactly right—and that if they do end up on the barbecue, it was at least a little bit their fault. (Never mind how problematic it is to compare human women to steaks or burgers or anything else that's for *consumption.*) Theologies of female modesty are the primary evangelical Christian vehicle for *victim-blaming* in our churches today. And as we will see with each theology I explore in this book, this is a *feature* of the theology, not a *bug* or a *glitch.* This is how it is designed.

But modesty isn't applied equally to everybody. While it's rarely applied to men, it sometimes is, especially when church leaders want to pay lip service to the idea that they are not singling out women specifically with their modesty rules. Men also tend to suffer in communities with a heavy emphasis on modesty theology because the phrase "visual creatures" acts as a euphemism for "out-of-control sex monsters," and I've talked to many men who grew up in purity culture who struggled with self-hatred and low self-esteem for years because they believed that their very normal sexuality was fundamentally evil and broken. Additionally, not all women experience the teachings of modesty in the same way. It's difficult to enforce consistently because of things like climate, changing fashion norms, and the ever-evolving landscape of the Christian publishing industry that launches one book into fame and then another. But it's also difficult to enforce because no two bodies are the same, and different bodies experience different degrees of privilege, even—and perhaps especially—in church.

—

"So which is it?" Charlotte asked me over Skype one chilly October morning. "Am I too dangerous? Or do I just not exist?"

She was telling me about her experiences with modesty theology as a fat[4] Black woman growing up in the Assemblies of God church, describing how, because of her body size, church leaders made her feel simultaneously like no one would want her and like she had to cover up her body because it was too sexual. "I grew up with a lot of body hatred and internalized fatphobia along with the purity culture stuff," she told me. "It really seemed to go hand in hand."

Charlotte's stories only served to confirm what I'd been telling people for a long time: that it's really only possible for white women to "win" at purity culture.

"Black women are already hypersexualized anyway, going all the way back to slavery, and when you have a bigger body, it's even worse because people automatically assume you're sexual just because you have a big chest or big hips," she said. "The combination of being Black and then being fat on top of that means you're seen as somebody that just wants to, like, have sex all the time. Just based on how you look. It had nothing to do with how I acted. I was actually really shy."

Charlotte told me that during the peak of her modesty years, when she was still dutifully following all the "rules" her parents and her church had set for the appropriate way for women to dress, she still experienced sexual harassment and even sexual assault. The baggiest jeans and T-shirts did nothing to protect her from unwanted advances or men with bad intentions—and that included at church. And what happened when the worst-case scenario came true?

"Modesty teachings led to a lot of victim-blaming," Charlotte said before I could even ask her that question. "Because with the assault, it was like, *Oh it's your fault. You weren't dressed properly.*"

"Someone told you that?" I clarified.

"There was one instance from college I was thinking of in particular," she said, "when I was being harassed by this guy, and my friend said it was my fault because I was wearing a low-cut shirt. And that stuck with me for a really long time." Charlotte sighed. "But that's the thing about modesty being used as victim-blaming. Eventually you'll internalize it and then turn it on yourself. And then you don't even have to have people say it to you." Charlotte was right. Modesty theology becomes most powerful and most insidious when girls and young women have so internalized its messaging that they begin to self-police, no longer needing parents or church leaders to tell them to cover up because they have bought into the lie that it is their job to dress a certain way in order to avoid being "thrown on the barbecue."

As Charlotte and I talked, I was taken back to my own "goth phase" in junior high and early high school. Well, I don't know if I should call it a "phase," since now, at thirty years old, I have a sleeve and a half of tattoos and seven piercings, and as I write this paragraph, I am currently dressed completely in black—you can take the girl out of goth, but you can't take the goth out of the girl, as the saying goes. But I remember conversations in junior high between my parents where they were trying to decide whether they would allow me to "express myself" in this way. My mother was uncomfortable with it from an aesthetic standpoint, but I vividly remember my father specifically saying to her, "She's being modest. She's covered from head to toe. In black, but she's covered."

As I go back and read my journals from that time, there's a very obvious fixation present on not being like "those girls." I was using the word *preppy*, but what I really meant, but didn't know the word for at the time (because I was home-schooled), was *slutty. Those girls* who just let it all hang out and flirt with boys effortlessly and aren't very nice to me. *Those girls* who shop at Abercrombie & Fitch and actually have boyfriends and probably aren't even kissing virgins. I had so internalized the modesty = good girl and immodesty = bad girl messaging at such an early age that it made more sense to me to differentiate myself by wearing nothing but baggy black clothes for several years in hopes that it would signal to others not only my uniqueness but also my *virtue.* (I was also straight-up terrified of other girls on account of being gay, but that's a story for another chapter.)

"I think modesty is often used as an excuse to not believe victims," Charlotte said near the end of our conversation.

"What do you think that does to the idea of consent?" I asked.

"Well, it didn't matter whether or not I was comfortable with it," she said. "I had to do what the church and my parents said. So my ability to even consent to how I wanted to look was taken away."

—

By now, it should be fairly obvious that "Dress modestly so you don't cause your brother in Christ to sin" is one side of the coin, and "She was asking for it because she was dressed immodestly" is the other. And while many modesty proponents would probably reject that characterization, the fact that they would reject it in name doesn't mean it's not true. My aim here isn't to make people comfortable; it's to hold up a mirror. Moreover, I'm less interested in what people claim to believe and more interested in what they actually do. As we'll see with this and so many of the other doctrines in the chapters that follow, there is often a vast chasm between those two.

When you look at the popular literature of modesty theology in the evangelical church today, scary barbecue metaphors from misogynists with frosted tips aside, it's often framed in terms of *female empowerment*. In fact, many writers even co-opt the language of feminist theory to claim that what they are doing actually fights objectification, presumably because if you are modestly covered, nobody can objectify you. They claim that secular (read non-Christian) culture is "obsessed with sex," and by dressing modestly, women can opt out of that game and focus on letting men get to know them for their characters rather than their bodies.

In *Every Young Woman's Battle: Guarding Your Mind, Heart, and Body in a Sex-Saturated World* (one book in a series that frames sexuality as warfare—*Every Woman's Battle*, *Every Man's Battle*, and *Every Young Man's Battle* are some of the other titles), authors Shannon Ethridge and Stephen Arterburn state, "If you want to be a young woman of sexual integrity, you will be different. Smarter. You will teach your guy friends how to treat you with dignity and respect rather than teaching them that you are eye candy or a toy for their sexual jollies."[5] Integrity. Smarter. Dignity. Respect. Look at all that empowering language!

Flip back a few pages, however, and you'll see Ethridge and Arterburn sharing the story of a young woman who was a camp counselor for girls at a Christian camp. The woman relays the story of how, in an attempt to connect with her young campers and make them think she was cool, she pushed the limit on what was considered acceptable, "modest" dress for camp employees.

She says, "[Male colleagues] chased me around with water guns, gave me piggyback rides to the cafeteria, slipped ice down the back of my shirt, and fun stuff like that. I kept asking them to please leave me alone so I could concentrate on my girls, but they rarely respected my requests, no matter how firm I was. I complained to one of the other counselors about how the guys were distracting me from what I came to do. She put her hand on mine and sweetly said, 'Christi, your actions speak louder than your words. . . . If you dress like a cute little plaything and present yourself as a toy, then boys will be boys and try to play with that toy!'"[6]

So, um. *taps mic* Is this thing on? That is *sexual harassment.* If you put ice cubes down the back of a woman's shirt, and she firmly asks you to stop, and then you keep doing it anyway . . . that's sexual harassment. But instead of this tale being a lesson in the way that sexual harassment often goes underreported and underprosecuted in religious environments, it's presented as a lesson of "Well? What did you expect? You *were* dressed like a plaything, after all." Only people aren't toys, and sexual harassment isn't a game. So much for female empowerment in a "sex-saturated world." Where's all that dignity talk now?

While many of the modesty gurus of purity culture claim that "the world" is "obsessed with sex," I would argue that purity culture in general and modesty theology specifically betray an equally fierce yet complementary obsession with sex compared with what is found in broader, non-Christian society. Obviously, many secular institutions are wildly exploitative of women's sexuality in the opposite direction—whittling women's worth down to how hot and sexy their bodies are, how young and youthful they can appear, or how well they can approximate the aesthetic values of whiteness and heterosexuality. But whittling women's worth down to how modest and covered they are is *not* the answer and is equally objectifying and exploitative.

There are those who, when confronted with all of this information about the fallout of modesty theology, will still claim that teachings about modesty have nothing to do with the problem of sexual assault and harassment in the church. To that I would say that only those with vested financial and social interest in the propagation of purity culture seem to be mysteriously unable to connect the dots. Christian modesty theology actively, demonstrably plays a part in blaming survivors for their own harassment, abuse, and assault—by definition. There is no way to teach that women must obligatorily dress "modestly" (however each individual community defines that) for the sake of men without also implying the inherent guiltiness of women who do not comply or who fail to meet the standard. The way that modesty theology has played a part in hundreds and thousands of survivors' stories should put to shame anyone who ever promoted it to their daughters, wives, congregants, or youth group students. As Jessica Valenti points out in her seminal work *The Purity Myth*, "So long as women are supposed to be 'pure,' and so long as our morality is defined by our sexuality, sexualized violence against us will continue to be both accepted and expected."[7]

—

It was 2011, and my family had come to visit me in Chicago for the weekend while I was a junior at Moody Bible Institute. On Sunday morning, I took them to my church with me—a reformed, neo-Calvinist Acts 29 church on the north side I had only started attending to flirt with a boy who had long since chosen someone else. But I had other friends who went there, and I got sucked in by the community, and I didn't want to be that person that only went to a church for a boy, so I stayed. (I also had a brief love affair with Calvinism as a Moody student. What can I say? Certainty is a hell of a drug, and they were writing prescriptions for it left and right at bible college.) We sat in the balcony that morning, in two rows to accommodate our large group. The worship band wandered onto the stage and began to pick up their instruments and plug in their microphones, as the service was about to begin.

As the first song started, my mother suddenly whipped her head around from the row in front of me and tried to speak just loud enough to be heard over the music: "Who is *that?*" she asked. My eyes darted toward the stage, and I immediately knew who she was talking about: the lead female singer, standing just to the left of center stage. She was wearing a bright pink skirt that fell just above her knees and a bright yellow top that hugged her body's curves and showed a sliver of belly and cleavage, with velvety, knee-high boots completing the outfit. Her radiant colors were in stark contrast to the men in the worship band all around her, dressed in neutral T-shirts and blue jeans. I could tell from my mother's face that this was not a positive question. I panicked.

"I—uh," I stammered. "I think she's a new Christian."

This seemed to satisfy her. "Hmm," she said, the corners of her mouth turning down in a shrug. "She better be." She turned back around and sang along with the song, mollified for the time being.

My mother may have been satisfied, but I was anything but. I could barely concentrate the rest of the service. I have never forgotten the way I threw that other woman under the bus to my mother for the sake of upholding modesty theology, and I have never stopped being sorry for it. The thing is, I think she *had* just become a Christian. But it shouldn't have mattered. There was nothing wrong with what she was wearing because there was nothing wrong with her body. Her outfit made perfect sense for a balmy spring morning in Chicago in a gathering full of young millennials in a repurposed theater. But she didn't meet the criteria in at least one person's mind, so instead, her choices had to be explained away as those of a "baby Christian." Why else would someone be so reckless and immodest? Hopefully as she grows and matures in Christ, she'll learn not to dress so sluttily, for the sake of the men in the room.

You see how it goes.

The reason I started my analysis of purity culture and #ChurchToo with modesty is because it's the most surface-level doctrine—but it's also the most insidious. It worms its way into the minds of women and men alike, convincing them that anything a woman might wear could affect her value, worth, and dignity. It is the first way we learn in Christian community to blame victims—and the first way Christian women learn to blame themselves. It's an outward signifier that Christian leaders believe they can point to that supposedly indicates a woman's purity and virtue. It is the very currency of rape apologism in churches.

And as we'll see in the chapters that follow, modesty doesn't work alone.

3

THE WORKS OF THE FLESH

Now the works of the flesh are obvious: fornication, impurity,
licentiousness . . .

—Galatians 5:19

If this were a different sort of book, I might start this chapter by launching straight into a discussion of the fraught
hermeneutical issues inherent in translating a Greek word
like πορνεία (*porneia*) into the English word *fornication*. I
might talk about how that choice on the part of translators
betrays more ideological commitment than it does knowledge of biblical languages or the concept creep (there's that
pesky phenomenon again) of the word *fornication* itself. I
might even attempt to tell you "what the bible actually says"
about "sex before marriage."

But this is not that sort of book.

You can find those books in the appendix in the back, and if you're a person who identifies as a Christian and views the bible as an important source of guidance and authority for life, you'll definitely want to check them out. But I also recognize that not all of you will fall into that category, and moreover, I'm not sure as finite human beings that we have access to "what the bible actually says" any more than we have access to what any text "actually says." James K. A. Smith, whose body of work and terrible behavior on Twitter I don't necessarily endorse, taught me early on in his book *The Fall of Interpretation* that objectivity is a myth for people desperate for security and that we can never truly transcend the interpretive space—or skip interpretation—to arrive at pure, unadulterated meaning.[1]

I'm not trying to ignite an existential crisis for anyone, but the question of "what the bible says about premarital sex" is one I get asked ad nauseam. And what I've learned from trying to answer it hundreds of times is that trying to make a claim about "what the bible actually says" is itself an act of interpretation. There is no such thing as "noninterpreted" biblical truth. To quote Wesley from the classic movie *The Princess Bride*, "Anyone who says differently is selling something." We are all, always, interpreting. And so rather than making a claim about what the bible "actually says" about nonmarital sex, I'm going to explore what certain people *say* the bible says—their interpretations—and the very real and undeniable ties those interpretations have to the crisis of #ChurchToo.

—

In the late 1990s and early 2000s, when many #ChurchToo survivors were growing up in evangelical Christian homes and churches, countless books and events and nonprofit organizations were dedicated to making sure we all knew that God and our families and our churches expected us to refrain from having any kind of sex until we were legally married to someone who had also done the same. By this time, the purity movement had taken off, and millions of federal and state dollars were being allocated each year to abstinence-only education (more on this in chapter 5).

But arguably one of the most influential books of that era was the now infamous *I Kissed Dating Goodbye*,[2] written by evangelical homeschooler Joshua Harris and published in 1997, when he was just twenty-one years old—and single. *I Kissed Dating Goodbye* parroted many of the standard purity culture messages that by its publication had become widespread in churches everywhere—save sex for marriage, the bible says so; if you don't follow the rules, you'll put yourself in danger of negative consequences; and so on. But Harris's interpretation of these supposedly divine statutes also added layers of concern around *dating*—a word he used throughout the book to refer to romantic relationships that feature emotional intimacy and physical interaction of almost any kind. Harris advocated for parentally supervised "courting" instead and lauded what came to be known as "emotional purity," which meant being sure to save not just your body but your heart for your theoretical future spouse as well. Harris, who announced his own divorce and deconversion on Instagram in 2019,[3] promised that following these guidelines would ensure that you would be able to enter into a lifelong, happy marriage with as little baggage as possible.

Harris may have been a virtual celebrity when I was growing up, but ultimately the success and rapid spread of Harris's no-dating theology wasn't about Harris himself. He was in the right place at the right time, publishing a book in 1997 as millions of federal dollars were being funneled into the cause he was championing and churches everywhere were glomming onto the purity message like the sticky tape in their favorite metaphors for soiled women. Lots of older adults whose prefrontal cortexes were fully formed decided to promote the ideas of a single twenty-one-year-old with no formal theological training, which allowed him to influence millions of young people and their parents with his untested theories. All of this was before Harris had come forward and shared with the world that he himself was a victim of childhood sexual abuse.[4] Years later, allegations of covered-up sexual abuse at the church Harris pastored would arise—allegations that Harris has still not, in his recent apology tour,[5] addressed sufficiently for survivors.[6] But at the time, Harris's message spread like wildfire, and his communication skills paired with a controversial book title put the precepts of *I Kissed Dating Goodbye* on par with the bible in many communities.

It wasn't just Harris, though. The 1990s and early 2000s were a dream market for writers publishing books that claimed that sex before marriage is a sin. Parents and churches couldn't eat them up fast enough.

In *When God Writes Your Love Story*, married authors Eric and Leslie Ludy claim that "God has set up a clear pattern for beautiful romance. We cannot experience the kind of love, sex, and intimacy we long for unless we follow His pattern. And His pattern is purity. Following His pattern means living in absolute faithfulness—body, mind, and heart—to one person for a lifetime. It means honoring God's marriage covenant as sacred and saving every expression of sexual intimacy for *after* the covenant wedding vows are spoken."[7] *Every Young Woman's Battle*, the book I quoted in chapter 2, states that "God's perfect plan is that you enjoy sexual intercourse exclusively within marriage. . . . The great sex you and your husband will enjoy someday will be free from painful consequences or guilt—and well worth the wait!"[8] Mary A. Kassian, in her book *Girls Gone Wise in a World Gone Wild*, writes that "we honor God with our sexuality by restricting physical, sexual expressions of intimacy to the confines of marriage, and by delighting in the joy of marital sex. Keeping sex exclusive to the marriage covenant and having great sex with one's spouse, is the right way for Christians to display the purity, unity and fidelity of the church's relationship to Christ."[9]

Quite a consistent tune they're all singing, no? And these are just the books I happened to have on my shelf. There are dozens more, and you can find them with a quick Google search or a jaunt over to your local Christian bookstore. But there's just one problem.

The sexual ethics they recommend are really, really unhealthy.

—

"Unless abstinence is their decision—unless it's 100 percent their decision—it's never not going to be shaming," Dr. Tina Schermer Sellers said to me over Skype while I was huddled away in a coworker's office to take the midmorning call. Dr. Sellers had been telling me about this straight couple she knew that, for creativity's sake, had decided to abstain from intercourse for as long as they could and learn how to have great sex in every other way—and how amazing that had been for them and how what they learned through that time had continued to serve them well throughout their now ten-year marriage. This kind of freely chosen and shame-less abstinence is a far cry from the "choice" many young people make today—one where they are told they can "choose" to be abstinent, but if they don't make that choice, they will anger God and their parents and end up miserable and alone. I question what kind of "free choice" can possibly be made in a world where any other choice means that one's spiritual community, quality of living, and potentially even financial security and housing may be at risk. I have known more than one person who became homeless or was at risk of homelessness because they lived with their parents, and their parents disapproved of their "lifestyle choices."

But ultimately, Dr. Sellers said, we need to get honest about one thing: purity culture *isn't working*. At least not the way parents and pastors want it to. "Statistics will tell you the average adolescent is having sex. And that's any genital contact, but they're having sex somewhere between sixteen and seventeen, give or take. By the time they're eighteen to twenty years old, it's 80 percent who are sexually active. And this includes fundamentalist evangelical conservatives," she said.

"Those who have been through True Love Waits and done the purity pledges," I said with a wry smile.

"Yeah," Dr. Sellers continued. "For evangelicals, the average age is 16.9. And our conservative kids are using less contraception, and they have higher STI and pregnancy rates."

So all this work—all these purity programs and youth group retreats and abstinence swag and millions of federal and state dollars being poured into funding this industry—isn't actually preventing young or unmarried people from having sex, which is, like, kind of the whole point. So *what is it doing?* Are there any good outcomes? Even intangible or emotional outcomes?

One of the mythical promises of purity culture is that following its precepts will result in a happy, healthy, thriving romantic life with one's future spouse when you do eventually get married. You'll be much happier, so the logic goes, than those who made lots of sexual and romantic connections with others before marriage because you'll have saved all that connection and sexual energy for one person.

"Do people end up having healthier lives, healthier bonding, when they follow that line of living? When they attach, does it amount to them having a more flourishing, thriving sexual life? Is that what we end up seeing? The answer is no," Dr. Sellers stated matter-of-factly. And she would know. She sees the relational casualties of purity culture in her office all the time. These couples, she said, are "attempting to do a relationship where she's been taught it's all about him, and *he's* been taught it's all about him, and now they enter into a transactional sexual relationship where nothing about her pleasure is being considered, she knows nothing about her own body, he knows nothing about her body, and she's just handing over her body to him."

I nodded soberly, thinking of how many of my friends from college had reached their wedding night with high hopes only to have them dashed during the first few weeks and months of marriage when purity culture failed to make good on its lofty promises. Young women fresh out of purity culture were left to navigate their new relationships with their husbands and their new relationships with their bodies completely alone. I never heard the word *clitoris* until I was twenty-one, and only then because of Google. Purity culture involves very little instruction about *pleasure*, and when it does acknowledge pleasure at all, it is either to remind married Christians struggling in their sex lives that pleasure is not the point (obedience to God is) or to remind wives that pleasure is something they owe their husbands, regardless of how they personally feel about sex.

I thought of my own experience with my ex-husband. We had started dating after I theoretically didn't think premarital sex was a sin anymore, but we still waited until we'd been dating for a year to have intercourse, in large part because I wasn't ready to apply the same sexual freedom I gave to others to myself. I had also never had a sexual partner, but he had, and he was more than happy to wait until I was ready. I thought of how precious that time was and how thankful I was to have been with someone who supported me in my desire to take things slowly, at my own pace, and choose the right time for me and for us to take that step. One hundred percent our decision, just like Dr. Sellers said.

I'm convinced there's a connection between abstinence-only teachings and the crisis of #ChurchToo—and between purity culture and a culture of abuse. But I wanted to hear Dr. Sellers's take. "You tell a child 'don't think, don't feel, don't do,'" she said, "and if you do any of those things, then all this bad will happen. And you've given them no knowledge. You've given them no resources, nothing to equip them to protect themselves. So they have nothing. And then you send them out into the world, and they are as naked as they can be. They cannot protect themselves. And you are now no longer a resource, because you've made it clear that if they come to you, you'll only punish them. So now they're out in this world where there is exploitation at every turn. And they can't recognize the exploitation because you've given them no tools to recognize the exploitation. They can't differentiate fantasy from reality, because they don't know the difference. It's like throwing your children to the wolves. You've just done that."

I sat in silence for a few moments on the other end of the Skype call, stewing in the truth of her words. The inability to differentiate fantasy from reality had played more than a small part in my own experience of abuse in the church—as had the knowledge that parents and pastors could not be trusted because they would only punish me for straying outside the expected norm if I asked the wrong questions or revealed too much. In other words, the threat of sexual shame kept me quiet.

"I don't think that there is a greater way that you can hurt people than sexual shame," Dr. Sellers said. "And it is why sexual shame looks so much like sexual abuse. Because it *is* sexual abuse."

—

In my conversation with Dr. Sellers, I learned that we didn't have a clinical, operational definition of what exactly sexual shame was until 2017—when Noël Clark, a PhD student at Seattle Pacific University, wrote her doctoral dissertation, "The Etiology and Phenomenology of Sexual Shame: A Grounded Study Theory."[10] Over the course of writing this dissertation, which I am forever indebted to Dr. Sellers for sending me, Clark did a qualitative research study and interviewed women who had experienced sexual shame as well as therapists who work with those who have experienced sexual shame. The definition she came up with is absolutely stunning: "Sexual shame is a visceral feeling of humiliation and disgust toward one's own body and identity as a sexual being, and a belief of being abnormal, inferior and unworthy. This feeling can be internalized, but also manifests in interpersonal relationships, having a negative impact on trust, communication and physical and emotional intimacy. Sexual shame develops across the lifespan, in interactions with interpersonal relationships, one's culture and society, and subsequent critical self-appraisal."[11]

Clark goes on to say that sexual shame negatively affects people's ability to make decisions for themselves in sexual relationships as well as their feelings about whether they even have the power or the knowledge to make such decisions. Her analysis confirms what I have been saying for a long time—that purity culture, contra its claims, doesn't actually teach young people to say no. It just teaches them to say nothing. Teaching them to say no would be teaching them to hold a personal boundary. And it's dangerous to teach people whose obedience you are trying to ensure, especially young women, to hold personal boundaries. If you teach someone to say no, the next thing you know, they might be saying yes because they might think they deserve to have a say in what happens to them. Far safer to get them to say nothing at all.

Shame is a perfect tool to keep someone quiet. Shame and silence walk hand in hand, and they open the door for abuse. As Dr. Sellers put it, "Shame makes us feel like this power in us, this desire in us, is really bad. So anything that's related to that shame goes deeper and deeper into secrecy inside of us. And when that shame gets tapped in on, whether that's by a boyfriend or girlfriend or whether it's by someone who's exploiting us, we can't tell the difference. Because we're already sure it's always been our fault. We are bad. It's always been us. It's always been because of us."

—

Noël Clark may have only written her doctoral dissertation in 2017, but so much of the other information I've presented here—data on the ineffectiveness of purity pledges, the higher rates of STIs and unintended pregnancies among young people raised in purity culture, the negative effect of shame on self-esteem and a personal sense of autonomy—has all been around for many years and is easily available to anyone with access to Google. Purity culture has *been* not working. So why do Christian pastors and youth pastors and parents keep digging their heels in and teaching it to our young people year after year, even when all the best and most reliable evidence suggests that this theology makes them vulnerable not only to exploitation but also to all kinds of negative mental and physical health outcomes?

The answer is complicated.

Some of it goes back to the bible. Some parents and pastors truly believe that this is what the bible requires of them, for a myriad of reasons. At best, I believe they are misguided, reading the bible with what I call an "Amelia Bedelia hermeneutic" that requires taking everything in the text literally, with little to no analysis for context clues or historical significance.

Some of it is because evangelical Christian culture has a well-documented and dangerous pathology of external or "secular" bodies of knowledge. It's the same reason Christian schools and Christian music and Christian science museums and Christian insurance companies exist: because secular authorities cannot be trusted. You only need to look at the number of antivaccination activists who are also conservative Christians to see how many Christians are primed to distrust and dismiss sound medical and scientific information if it does not come from their list of preapproved sources.

Still more of it has to do with fear. The culture of evangelical Christianity as a whole does not do well with negative emotions and has a vicious love affair with certainty, telling you that if you only do the right things and say the right prayers and believe the right theologies, you can be sure you won't burn in hell forever. Purity culture is similar. The idea that if you are abstinent until marriage, you won't get hurt and you'll enter marriage happy and whole is enticing. But it's simply not true. I am all for improving the quality of what we teach our children, which is one reason I wrote this book, but nothing we teach them can insulate them from pain in life. That is a pipe dream.

But the real answer, I think, is the self-reinforcing system of purity culture itself. Communities and families that practice purity culture usually leave a little wiggle room for ideological and doctrinal disagreement in other areas. All but the most hardline neo-Calvinists usually have some tolerance for the "free will" versus "divine plan" conversation, for example. And the debate over what kinds of music and movies are appropriate for Christians (as long as there are no visible breasts, of course) allows for more than one viewpoint. Most communities make room for varying beliefs on pneumatology, anthropology, ecclesiology, eschatology, and more. But when it comes to sex, all that grace for varying opinions goes out the window.

Purity culture is not just a self-reinforcing system but a *self-policing* one. As soon as you start to let on that *maybe* you don't believe premarital sex is a sin, *maybe* you're rethinking your stance on LGBTQ rights, or *maybe* the folks on the pro-choice side have some good points—then people come out of the woodwork to draw you back into the fold by whatever means necessary, no matter how invasive or unflinchingly cruel they have to be. I've previously mentioned public figures like Jennifer Knapp, Jen Hatmaker, and others who were summarily crucified in the digital public sphere for all to see, serving as an example that this too shall happen to you if you stray. But this happens in churches and even families in a smaller way every day. Every community has a scapegoat. Every community has a heretic whom those left behind use as an example of what you must never become.

In my experience, many parents and pastors and youth leaders are utterly *terrified* to publicly question the precepts of purity culture. I know because they're in my inbox constantly telling me about it. For the first few years of my public speaking career, most of my gigs were arranged by pastors who wanted to raise the questions I was raising and have the discussions I was facilitating but didn't want to get fired. One of them still did after I came and spoke at his church.

The consequences of questioning the sacrosanctity of purity culture are severe. You can lose your friends and your respect in the community. If you're employed by a church or a Christian school, you run the risk of losing your job. You lose your privacy and your peace online as your inboxes and DMs fill up with former friends calling you names and insulting your intelligence and implying threats about your eternal destiny. You might even lose your family. I did.

—

The other day I forgot to bring my potted basil plant in for the night when there was a frost advisory. I woke in the morning and found the plant drooping and withered, splotched brown where moisture in the leaves had frozen overnight. I felt horrible. I put the plant in the sun, tried watering it, watering it again, bringing it inside—and nothing. It couldn't recover, as hard as I tried.

Most of my biological family hasn't spoken to me in several years because of the way that I have unapologetically rejected purity culture and tried to help others do the same. Our fragile, wounded relationship never recovered from the way they mishandled my abuse and moved on as if nothing had happened, and like my poor basil plant, no amount of nurturing, no amount of *trying* could change what had happened—and what was continuing to happen. I wouldn't even write about this in a book except that it's been so long now that I have lost hope of reconciliation, and I am trying to say that *I have skin in this game*. Family means everything to me, and I lost one of the most important things in my life because my principles mean more to me than keeping people happy by maintaining the status quo. I understand that under a system like purity culture, it is terrifying to change your mind and even more terrifying to communicate to others that you have changed your mind. I deeply, deeply empathize with the risks involved. Sometimes the worst does happen. Sometimes your nightmares come true.

I will also say this: I have never, not even for one single second, regretted it. I have never regretted doing the right thing or fighting for the health and wholeness of others even when it causes me pain and puts me at significant personal risk. I have lost nothing that I needed, because I had it all inside me. And the people that have now become my precious, chosen family are people I would never have met if I hadn't been walking this path.

All that is to say that rejecting purity culture and abstinence-only theology is a moral imperative. But just because it is required does not mean it is easy. It requires parents and pastors and youth pastors and teachers and theologians to cultivate the emotional and spiritual resiliency necessary to be wrong and endure criticism and loss. But we have to do it. There is no other option. There is no deal to be made with the devil.

I hear the pain and fear in the voices of parents and youth leaders when they message me or raise their hands in a crowd and ask me, "How can I teach my kids to stay abstinent until marriage without shaming them / making them experience all the negative consequences of purity culture?" And I'm immediately taken back in time to this metaphor my mother always used to use when my siblings and I were young and we wanted to watch a movie. "Are there swear words in it?" she would ask. "Only one or two!" us kids would promise, several of our voices blending together into a chorus in the key of *whine*. "Well, while you watch the movie, I'll make you some brownies!" my mother would say. "And I'll just put a little bit of poop in them. Would that be OK?" On cue, we'd stick out our tongues and shout, "Yuck, no!"

Her point, however nonsensical when it came to cursing in movies, was that approaching the conversation from the place of "How much shit can I sneak into this?" was the wrong way to go about it. *How much purity culture can I sneak into my child's education without it actually being purity culture?* will never yield an education based on health, happiness, and consent. Purity culture is the disease, and the cure will never be more purity culture.

When I get that question, I usually sigh, take a big breath, and say something like, "Well, you can't. There's lots of data to support that. But we can talk about it. Thank you for asking. If you're asking questions, you're on the right track."

4

AT ALL TIMES

May her breasts satisfy you at all times;
may you be intoxicated always by her love.

—Proverbs 5:19

Do not deprive one another except perhaps by agreement for a set
time, to devote yourselves to prayer, and then come together again, so
that Satan may not tempt you because of your lack of self-control.

—1 Corinthians 7:5

When I was a student at Moody Bible Institute in Chicago, we were expected to go to chapel four times a week, where we sang worship songs, prayed, and listened to someone (almost exclusively men, usually white men) preach. We were expected to attend a church every Sunday in addition to school chapel, of course, but chapel was where we spent the bulk of our worshiping hours. Moody also required us to do multiple hours of off-campus volunteer work each week, and there were other mandatory activities, such as floor meetings, assigned accountability partners, and more. My entire life for those few years revolved around and was dictated by the school and its norms and expectations. It was my everything—my source of support, strength, community, and even income. In short, my bible college, like many Christian colleges, functioned in practice like, well . . . a big church.

We worshiped together. We prayed together. We served together. We ate together. We held each other accountable, participated in each other's lives, and did things recreationally together. As students, we were each other's whole worlds. Of course, Moody was careful to say that they weren't a church. After all, that's why we still had to go to church on Sundays and why women could be teachers (just not in the theology department). But the culture on campus was virtually the same as any large evangelical church you'd find anywhere in the country.

When we talk about #ChurchToo, it's very important to include Christian colleges in the analysis. Christian colleges are breeding grounds for the theologies that eventually become sacrosanct in our churches, and abuse and its mismanagement do not only occur out of ignorance. Far from it. Many pastors who commit abuse as well as cover it up are well educated and have degrees hanging on their walls from respected Christian schools. Like the Southern Baptist Convention, many would like to believe that the problem is "misapplied theology"—that if only these men had been taught the right theology or more correctly applied the theology they had been taught, we wouldn't be in this mess. But unfortunately, the facts do not bear that hypothesis out.

—

When #ChurchToo started going viral, survivors of abuse at Christian colleges began sharing their stories right alongside those who had experienced abuse in churches. I knew, both anecdotally and from my own experience at Moody, that abusive behavior was rampant and usually completely unchecked at most evangelical Christian colleges, and it was utterly unsurprising to me that many institutions were being implicated in the #ChurchToo fray. As students, we all knew who to stay away from in dimly lit hallways and parking lots. We all knew which professors got shuffled off to back offices where they'd have less face-to-face time with students. I knew someone in college who was stalked and harassed for weeks by her ex. The administration knew and did nothing. He's a youth pastor now.

But with the siren song of "misapplied theology" still ringing in my ears, I wanted to see, beyond anecdote, what these colleges were actually *teaching* about sexual abuse and assault. As the nonprofit organization Church Clarity[1] has taught us, there's no better way to see what an organization is teaching than by looking at its "actively enforced policies." Fortunately for my research, colleges are usually a lot more forthcoming than churches about what you can expect when you sign up.

In September 2019, I sent a tweet asking for people who had attended Christian colleges to send me copies of their codes of conduct—often going by names such as "student life guide," "behavior expectations," "community guidelines," and the like. Over 150 people responded and sent me documents from the schools they either attended in the past or were currently attending. And what I found going through them was both fascinating and disturbing.

I learned that my own alma mater, Moody Bible Institute, doesn't actually address sexual abuse or assault in its "Student Life Guide"[2] as of the 2019–20 school year—it merely refers readers to the standard Title IX policy on its website. I also learned that in the decade since my time there, they've added a "two-hour 'Informed U—Standing Together Against Sexual Violence and Misconduct' discussion-based session" for new students, the content of which, of course, wasn't detailed in the guide. Whatever that session teaches, though, obviously the employees of the institution needed it more than the students. In October of 2020 the public learned that the administration of Moody Bible Institute, including its Title IX office, had been covering up and quietly dismissing instances of sexual abuse, harassment, and assault on campus for years.[3] And many of the other schools I looked at didn't even get a brief seminar.

The University of Valley Forge is an Assemblies of God–affiliated school in Phoenixville, Pennsylvania. On page 14 of their student handbook, it states, "Members of the University community are required to refrain from all forms of sexual immorality including, but not limited to, any form of pornography, promiscuity, homosexuality, premarital sex, adultery, rape, sexual violence and abuse, public nudity, contact of intimate parts above or below clothing, sharing sexual images of oneself or others and other forms of sexual misconduct."[4] I'm not sure if the administrators of the University of Valley Forge genuinely believe that activities such as "pornography" or "contact of intimate parts above clothing" meet the legal criteria for "sexual misconduct" or if they are being willfully obtuse, but dealing with sexual assault in this way makes it clear that it carries the same moral weight as consensual sexual activity between two unmarried persons or two persons of the same sex, for example. And sadly, the University of Valley Forge is hardly alone.

Biola University's Undergraduate Student Handbook and Guide to University Policies, revised in 2015, lists sexual assault and harassment on page 6 in a list of prohibited behaviors that may warrant disciplinary action—directly above "sexual activity outside of marriage between a husband and a wife," "same-sex romantic behavior," and "persistent or exaggerated examples of cross-dressing."[5] At Florida College, a small Christian liberal arts school associated with the Church of Christ, sexual assault is a Category III offense and will cause the perpetrator to be automatically suspended—as will having sex outside of marriage, another Category III offense. These categories are laid out in an illustrative table and everything.[6] Bryan College in Dayton, Tennessee, famous for being the late progressive Christian author Rachel Held Evans's alma mater, states in its student handbook that sexual behavior outside of marriage is "prohibited even when consensual"[7]—leading readers to wonder why the writers of this handbook assume that the default for sexual activity is one of nonconsent and that consent is some kind of extra "garnish" sprinkled on top of a sexual experience that adds nothing to and takes nothing away from its morality.

Bob Jones University is certainly low-hanging fruit on the tree of my argument here, but their student handbook also states that "the Bible clearly prohibits not only nonconsensual sexual misconduct . . . but also any consensual sexual activity outside the boundaries of heterosexual marriage."[8] Given that much of the "sex" depicted in the bible appears to be nonconsensual or consent-ambiguous, I'm not sure how clearly the bible prohibits anything of the sort, but that's beside the point. Collapsing the very large moral difference between consensual sex and nonconsensual "sex," otherwise known as assault, makes consent a nonissue. It also incorrectly locates the offense in the body and in the interaction between bodies, further stigmatizing sex and fostering shame and silence.

For fruit a little higher on the tree, we can turn to Liberty University. At Liberty, the fine for getting caught undressed with the person you're dating ($150 and fifteen hours of community service) is the same as the fine for sexual assault and harassment. If the assault or harassment is considered bad enough, you can get up to a three-hundred-dollar fine with possible dismissal—but you can also get that for spending the night with someone of a different sex.[9] Considering that the now-disgraced former president of Liberty University, Jerry Falwell Jr., was recently forced to resign after it was revealed that he and his wife had been involved in a seven-year sexual and financial arrangement with a much-younger Miami pool boy,[10] I wonder what the fine is for that. (Lest you think Jerry Falwell is the only hypocrite here, his wife Becki has also now been accused of sexual assault by a former Liberty student.)[11]

I could go on. As I said, people sent me 150 of these. And the consistent theme that I see across almost every single one is that sexual abuse, assault, harassment, and all forms of sexual violence are considered to be just one of the many ways that people can "sin sexually" or break the rules about sex that the bible supposedly teaches. They all get swept up into this neat little pile labeled "sexual sin," and any real-life differences between the acts themselves are flattened out until you're just as much of a sinner if you give your fiancé a blow job two weeks before your wedding as you are if you stalk and rape a congregant in your spiritual care. Both of those sins put Jesus on the cross, after all.

Popular Christian purity literature reflects this inability to distinguish consensual sexual activity from assault and harassment as well. Think of the story from chapter 2 from *Every Young Woman's Battle*, where the young woman working at a Christian camp was being sexually harassed by her male coworkers, and yet it was her *immodesty* that was called out as sin. Joshua Harris in *I Kissed Dating Goodbye* tells the biblical story of David and Bathsheba from 2 Samuel 11 as one of adultery and not, as most biblical scholars recognize it, rape.[12] David and Bathsheba is a popular cautionary tale in a lot of purity literature, always focusing on what the couple (especially Bathsheba) could have done to avoid "sexual sin" and never on the fact that a woman in that culture could not, by any stretch of the imagination, have said no to the king. When I read the many purity culture books on my shelf, I'm struck by how many of the stories they tell about sex and sin and loss of "virginity" are actually stories of harassment, coercion, and abuse—but the authors don't even realize it.

Christian authors, pastors, teachers, speakers, parents, professors, and college administrators have a very big problem distinguishing consensual sexual activity from assault, harassment, and abuse. Moreover, I would go so far as to say that for many, consent is viewed as an irrelevant factor when evaluating the morality of any given sexual situation. I think often of that meme where a couple is cuddling in bed and both have little speech bubbles above their heads that say, "I consent!" Next to them is white Jesus, with a speech bubble above his head that says, "*I* don't!" The meme is titled "The Myth of Consensual Sex." There's often a subtitle that reads, "Isn't there someone you forgot to ask?"

And given what purity culture teaches about sex, it actually makes sense to disregard consent. If all sexual experiences outside of one cisgender heterosexual man and one cisgender heterosexual woman in a legal, monogamous, lifelong marriage are sin, then why would it make any difference whether someone "consented" or not? Consent isn't important to many conservative Christians because consenting to sin is a nonsensical idea in their worldview. To people with this belief system, consenting to sex, if it's not the "right" kind of sex, is as pointless as consenting to bank robbery or voter fraud. You're still doing the wrong thing.

This explains why a lot of Christian families, churches, and schools don't even teach about consent at all. I know I certainly didn't hear the word *consent* as it relates to sexual activity until I was in college, and even then it was on the internet and not a part of any formal education I received. As I was putting this chapter together, I ran a quick Twitter poll asking my followers who grew up in purity culture to tell me when they first were taught about consent. Of the 3,588 people who responded, 5 percent (or 179 people) told me they learned about it as a child between the ages of zero and twelve. Another 14 percent (or 502 people) learned about it as a teenager between the ages of thirteen and eighteen. Twenty-six percent (or 932 people) indicated that they learned about consent in college, and a staggering 55 percent of respondents (or 1,973 people) told me that they were never taught about consent growing up at all or had to teach themselves about it as an adult. A casual Twitter poll is obviously not peer-reviewed science, but these numbers are jarring if they're even remotely accurate. *Christian communities are not talking about consent.*

Twitter polls aside, I knew the lack of education about consent to be anecdotally true from my own upbringing and college experience as well as from many conversations with friends and acquaintances about purity culture. But I wanted to talk to others about their experiences, so I sat down with two incredible women from Into Account, a nonprofit organization specializing in survivor advocacy, as well as one of my friends who experienced sexual harassment at a conservative Christian college to hear what they had to say about the way consent is talked about—and enforced—in these environments.

—

My first interaction with Into Account was at an Alliance of Baptists conference called "Just Sex" at Vanderbilt University in Nashville in September 2018. My fiancée and I attended this conference as one of our early dating activities because nothing says romance to two analytical minds like attending a sex conference together. This was ten months after the launch of #ChurchToo, so when I saw there was a breakout session on church sexual abuse, I made it a point to attend. I was utterly blown away.

The presenter was Hilary Jerome Scarsella, who is the director of theological integrity for Into Account and holds a PhD in theological studies from Vanderbilt. She spoke eloquently about the practical and cultural factors that go into building a culture of abuse in religious environments, and at the end of her presentation, she distributed a handout that I have kept on my desk ever since and will continue to keep on my desk until I am no longer having conversations about church sexual abuse and sexualized violence—in other words, forever.

The handout, which is intended for churches and other Christian communities to reflect on their preparedness for handling instances of sexual violence, is three pages long and consists of four different sections. The first three are all practical in nature: reporting, responding, and accountability. They deal with questions like "Does your reporting process protect survivors' confidentiality?" "Do you know under what circumstances your community will and will not contact the police or other law enforcement in response to a sexual violence report?" and "Does your community proactively make [information about sexual violence committed] available to other communities of faith in which this individual might seek a future position of employment?"[13] Basically, it covers all the practical stuff that any faith community could ask themselves regardless of theological persuasion. But the last section deals with "preventative and transformative community practices," and this is where things get really interesting. Questions in this section include "Does consciousness of sexual violence show up in your worship practices?" "Does your community intentionally cultivate a queer-affirming and sex-positive culture and theology?" and "Does your community [cultivate this culture and theology] in age-appropriate ways in your children's programs?" When I saw that, I knew that I was looking at an organization that recognized the connection between purity culture and #ChurchToo.

I also knew Into Account worked with survivors at many Christian colleges as well as churches, so as I was preparing to write this chapter, I got on a Skype call with Hilary and the executive director of Into Account, Stephanie Krehbiel, who also holds a PhD. These are some seriously smart women.

"Our mission is to accompany survivors through whatever processes they want," Stephanie said at the beginning of our call.

"We're aware that sexual violence is not a strictly interpersonal issue between the person who has perpetrated assault and the person who has experienced it," Hilary clarified. "It is a social issue and a cultural issue, and so responses and interventions need to happen in community. There need to be spaces that take responsibility for accompanying survivors through processes of confrontation and looking for justice and whatever it is that the survivor needs in order to be well in the aftermath of what happened to them."

As we got to talking about the specifics of abuse that occurs in Christian and religious environments, Stephanie said, "Any time that there's sexual abuse in a religious context, there's a spiritual abuse component." Oftentimes, the people who are in positions of authority in those contexts are allergic to talking about accountability, she said. "They want to talk about healing, and they want to put accountability and healing in some sort of oppositional relationship. Which is bullshit. Obviously." They were speaking my language.

I asked Hilary and Stephanie specifically about the "preventative and transformative community practices" that they coach churches and schools in developing and why that's so important—why simply updating policies and procedures isn't enough to make sure that religious communities care well for survivors.

"A policy is just words on paper," Hilary answered. "Words are always interpreted. It doesn't matter how clear your policy is; the people who are responsible for carrying out that policy are going to have to make a hundred different decisions about precisely what the words mean in this particular situation. And interpretive decisions are always made according to the culture and theology of the place where they're being made." This means that if a church's theology teaches that women are weak and apt to lie about something like sexual assault for attention, then the people on the committee who make decisions about whether or not a survivor is telling the truth—and therefore whether there is anything to report—are going to be informed by that. If a Christian school teaches theology that says that LGBTQ persons are hypersexual and out of control, never being able to satisfy their ravenous desire to sin, then the administration is going to be considerably less likely to believe that an LGBTQ person could be a victim of assault. And if a Christian community believes that all sins are equal in the eyes of God and that the only true Christian posture toward someone who has wronged you is one of blanket forgiveness and openness to reconciliation, then survivors who are angry about what happened to them represent a threat even bigger than the sexual abuse itself.

"One thing that's really important," Hilary noted, "is whether a community regards a survivor who comes forward as being in need of saving or as being someone who has the potential to give the gift of wisdom and justice to the church. If you see a survivor as a prophet in the Christian narrative, you're going to engage your policy much differently than if you see a survivor as a wounded person in need of the moral exemplar of the church." Hilary's words rang true as I thought of the number of times in the two years since the launch of #ChurchToo that I had been accused by people I knew and strangers alike of trying to "destroy the church." Never mind that I still go to church. Never mind that I speak frequently at churches and Christian colleges. *Never mind that I work at a church for my actual job.* I'm gay and I'm angry and I'm loud, and I refuse to see myself in need of rescuing by the church, and I will not feign gratefulness for being invited to the table as an afterthought. Good evangelical Christian church leaders want nothing to do with me, and they make sure to tell me on the regular.

I'm in good company, though. "The charge that we get is, 'You say that you're helping survivors, but all you're doing is tearing us down!' That is a constant refrain for us," Stephanie said. This is especially true, she noted, in Christian colleges, where faculty, staff, administrators, and the community at large often have difficulty differentiating themselves from the institution.

"The Christian college sees itself as an incubator for the best of the best of the Christian church," Hilary observed. "Christian colleges see themselves as the trainers of the future of the church and the apex experts on what it means to be the church—and also the ones who are modeling the church better than the church itself." That was certainly true of how the student community and even many professors at Moody thought of themselves while I was there.

But when these colleges, like the ones I quoted a few pages back and so many others all across the country, treat sexual assault and harassment like just another prohibited sexual activity, things get even worse. "What happens when you've engaged in some of the prohibited sexual activities, and at some point you stop consenting and it turns into sexual assault?" Stephanie asked, letting the answer we all knew hang in the air for a few seconds before going on. "It's treated differently because the perception is that the person may have been sexually assaulted, but they also did prohibited sexual things, so all parties are going to be treated the same way."

"If you're actually interested in getting reports," she said, "treating sexual assault like yet another prohibited sexual activity is going to stop people from reporting." I wanted to get Stephanie's words tattooed on my forehead, or shout them from a mountaintop, or print them on business cards and mail them to every Christian college in the country. But on Christian college campuses, making it safe for people to report sexual assault or harassment is only a fraction of the battle. Getting the administration to believe the survivor or do anything about it? Well, that's a whole other story.

—

My friend Julia,[14] who now holds a master of social work and supervises a program that provides clinical interventions and case management services to adults living with severe mental illness, was a student at a prominent evangelical bible college from 2010 to 2012. She agreed to share her story with me for this book, so we sat down on Skype to talk about it. Julia told me that by the time she began working as an administrative assistant at one of the department offices on campus, she had already had several negative experiences with the way sexual assault and harassment were treated by students, faculty, and administration. But she had recently started dating her boyfriend, Greg, also a student at this same bible college, and she was very hopeful about their relationship. After they had been dating for a short time, Julia shared with him that she had been sexually assaulted in high school.

"From the get-go," Julia told me, "rather than responding as a significant other or even as a friend, he took on a very investigative persona. He was asking me questions like, 'Well, what do you *mean* you didn't want it?' 'Did you ever fight back? Like, physically, actually fight back?' 'If you didn't want it, why didn't you just tell someone right away?'" Things didn't stop there, though. "Throughout the course of the relationship, he would regularly say things like 'I just don't know if I can really commit to this, because it means that I have to maintain the sexual purity of our relationship, because you can't.' It was such a gaslighting experience," she reflected, "because he was accusing *me* of being someone who couldn't respect *his* boundaries."

As their relationship deteriorated, Greg's cruelty and sense of control over Julia and her life experience came to a head: "He would make statements like, 'A woman with a history of sexual abuse isn't what I envisioned for my future wife.' That was something he said a lot. There came a point where he became even more accusatory and told me he needed to know every little thing that ever happened between me and another man. He wanted *details*. I remember taking a notebook and writing down every sexualized encounter, consensual or not consensual, that I could remember having, even sexting, and giving that to him."

Greg's behavior was obviously extreme, but I also knew there were lots of Gregs out there. I myself had dated a guy at Moody who, when he broke up with me, told me that he expected over the course of his life that many women would want to sleep with him, so he needed to marry someone really hot so that he wouldn't be tempted to stray, and I just didn't fit the bill. So I asked her, "Do you think it was just Greg, or was that kind of the culture on campus?"

Julia paused. "Hmm," she began cautiously. "In mental health assessments, if we're describing things like speech or affect, a lot of times we'll write this phrase, 'within normal limits.' So while it was a little exaggerated with him, I feel like it was still within normal limits of the culture of the school. Like, I cannot imagine that any amount of education or socialization that he received there would have ever done anything to confront those beliefs or lead him to consider if they were wrong. I think it was a very enabling environment for the beliefs that he had." At this particular bible college, complementarianism[15] was the law of the land, women could not be pastors or even teach theology classes, and physical contact between nonmarried couples beyond holding hands and brief hugs was prohibited.

But while all of this was going on with Greg, Julia had also just started her new job. "I didn't even apply for that job," Julia told me. "I was brought on personally by Charles," the head of the department, a man in his late fifties who had daughters Julia's age. "There was a nonprofit that had come into one of the classes he taught to give a presentation, and I had volunteered to help with that, and after that he called me in and basically, with no knowledge of my work history or qualifications or experiences, offered me the job."

As soon as she started the job, the grooming began: "He started coming in several times a day while I was working, and from the start, he made a habit of closing the door to my office, even though it was always open. No other staff could see or hear what was going on because there wasn't a window." Then, she said, he began initiating physical touch in small, seemingly innocent ways: "If there was a hair or a fuzz or something on my body, he would reach over and pull it off of me. Eventually I tried to set a boundary about that because there were a couple of times when it really startled me."

Over time, the grooming behaviors started to increase as Charles broke bigger and bigger rules: "I ended up doing a lot of things in the office that I wasn't really supposed to be doing. I would regularly reconcile his budgets that weren't related to our office, and I pretty much taught his online classes for him. I especially wasn't supposed to be doing that, because he taught Acts online and a bunch of other biblical courses, and as a woman I wasn't allowed to teach those. So it was creating this relationship dynamic where we were doing something secretly together."

The summer after she started working in Charles's office, Julia went to Europe on a study-abroad trip. When she came back and returned to work, things got even worse. Charles would often travel to represent their bible college at other schools for admissions purposes, but there came a time when he had two back-to-back overnight engagements that he was not going to be able to attend. At this point, Julia and Greg had not yet broken up. "Charles asked me to go to these two events in his stead and said he figured I wouldn't want to go alone, so why don't I see if Greg can come. He offered to cover the car and the hotel for the night. He was literally suggesting I go on an overnight trip with my boyfriend"—something that could have gotten them both formally punished or even expelled had it been found out. Because of the risk, they declined.

But that didn't stop Charles from continuing to try to put Julia in a position of secrecy and indebtedness to him. "After Greg and I broke up, those ten- to fifteen-minute closed-door visits in my office became much longer and much more interrogative," Julia told me. "He was *convinced* I had an eating disorder even though I didn't. And any time I stood up for myself, he acted so hurt and sad and wounded. Shortly after I turned twenty-one, things took a turn for the worst."

Julia told me that she was accustomed by this point to Charles constantly leaving little gifts around the office for her. She said he even tried to buy her a new laptop once. But one day she walked into her office to find a note telling her where to look for the gift he had bought her this time. When she opened her desk drawer, she found a six-pack of beer and a carton of cigarettes. It was supposed to be a "joke" about Julia being an adult now, but she was livid. Students had gotten kicked out for drinking in the past, and possession on campus was a serious offense. "I didn't even smoke then. That was another situation where I got really, really angry and told him that it was completely unacceptable and inappropriate," she said.

Charles pressed on. He called Julia on her personal cell phone as late as 10:30 p.m., began sharing deeply intimate unsolicited details about his family and home life with her, and once even showed up at her dorm room door with flowers after her theater performance. Finally, he asked her to meet with him at a Starbucks off-campus to discuss his career at the college. Charles worked in two departments and was planning on resigning from one to focus on the other. "What did he say?" I asked Julia.

"He said he wanted to tell me because I was the only person he could talk to and I just 'got him,'" she said. "He expressed how glad he was that I was actually staying on campus and working this summer because he knew he wouldn't be able to get through the transition without me."

Summer and Charles's transition began. Julia was living on campus that summer for the convenience of being so close to work, and as such, she was receiving a discount on her housing. "That summer he was constantly asking me out for dinner and talking about how poor I was," Julia said. "I went a couple times when other people were also present just to get him off my back, but it was so awkward."

"But because he was leaving his job in the other department, he had to clean out his office, and he had me go over to the other building with him to help, sometimes for eight hours a day. By this point alarm bells were screaming in my head," Julia told me. She intuitively sensed that it was only a matter of time before things got much, much worse. She wanted to quit her job, but she also knew that if she quit, the school would rescind the discount she was receiving on her housing for the summer for working on campus, and she couldn't afford to pay full price. Finally, she talked to her dad and another close friend who had extensive work experience in the "secular" world. "They were horrified," Julia said. "They immediately told me I shouldn't have to quit my job and I should go to HR as soon as possible. They affirmed for me that what was happening was absolutely sexual harassment, and it wasn't appropriate or professional."

Unfortunately, the HR department at this particular bible college did not share the values of the "secular" world that Julia's dad and friend held. Julia sat down with a woman from HR for an extensive interview, and their initial recommendation was that she turn in her two weeks' notice while they did whatever they could do to ensure that her rent rate would not go up. However, shortly after the meeting, Julia received another email from her HR contact, instructing her to finish out the work week, go back to her dorm room on Friday evening, and send Charles an email letting him know that she was resigning effective immediately. After that email, she was to have no contact with him, and he was to have no contact with her. And she was expressly forbidden from speaking with *anyone* about the circumstances of her resignation.

"That's all I got," Julia said. "They didn't help me find a new job; they didn't place me in a new department. They did keep my rent from going up, but that didn't do much good when I was unemployed for the next month and lost about a thousand dollars in income I had been counting on."

As soon as Julia left, Charles hired another young female assistant in her position. As of the writing of this book, Charles still works at the college in the same office where he harassed Julia for so many months.

As Julia looks back on that time, she sees the college and its culture and administration as complicit in what happened to her. "He either thought that everything he was doing was completely acceptable, or he was absolutely a very skilled predator, especially when it came to grooming. But either way, he was working in an environment where he knew nothing was going to happen to him because of his actions." I made an off-handed comment about the HR department not viewing Julia as a reliable narrator of her own experiences, and she quickly corrected me. "No, that's the thing," she said. "I actually *do* think they thought I was a reliable narrator of my own experience. I think they thought I was telling the truth. I just don't think they cared. It was easier for them to tell me as a student to quit my job and assume that would remove any issues or liability."

But the real liability is still lurking within their walls.

—

According to Dr. Tina Schermer Sellers, whom I spoke to in the previous chapter, by the time young people are eighteen to twenty years old, 80 percent of them are sexually active—including young evangelical Christians who are abstinence-only educated and take purity pledges and, yes, even go to bible college. And it should scare everyone that the message these sexually active young people are receiving through their "Christian education" is that sexual assault, harassment, and abuse are morally equivalent to letting your hand slip while making out—it's all just "messing up" sexually. It takes two to mess up sexually—and often, in the minds of those influenced by purity culture, it takes two when it comes to sexual assault, harassment, and abuse.

Do you know what these "student life guides" and "codes of conduct" I was sent don't discuss? Consent. Not a single one outlines what does and does not constitute consent in a sexual situation. Not a single one attempts to prepare students,

80 percent of whom (at least) are having sex, for the situations they will face. Rather, they lump all sexual behavior that does not occur in the context of a legal monogamous marriage between a man and a woman into one category as "sin" and all sexual behavior that does occur in that context into another category as "holy." (This categorization says nothing about the fact that marital rape exists, which I will discuss in another chapter.)

It is little wonder that #ChurchToo is a veritable epidemic on Christian college campuses today. The bible itself says very little about consent, and the verses quoted in the epigraph of this chapter have been weaponized frequently to flatten out the need for consent in sexual relationships. The very idea of consent is often viewed as a liberal machination that no one would have any need for if they just followed the precepts of purity culture and waited until marriage.

But these very attitudes are tragically killing people. The base of any sexual ethic that honors and values the human person is and must be consent. Without consent—without the affirmation that human beings are allowed to say yes and no to the sexual experiences they do and do not desire—sex becomes a game of power, a contest where certain parties "win" and others "lose." And these attitudes about sex undergird a culture where vulnerable people are routinely taken advantage of and abuse is the rule rather than the exception. So many people wring their hands when confronted with the facts of #ChurchToo and wonder, *How did we get here?* For those whose eyes are open, the utter failure of purity culture to teach an entire generation the most basic component of ethical sex is not difficult to see.

5

NOT EVEN A HINT

> But among you there must not be even a hint of sexual immorality, or
> of any kind of impurity, or of greed, because these are improper for
> God's holy people.
>
> —Ephesians 5:3 NIV

When former kidnapping victim turned child safety advocate Elizabeth Smart spoke at a human trafficking conference at Johns Hopkins University in May 2013, she specifically mentioned the impact the sex education she received had on the way she viewed herself after being raped for nine months during her captivity: "[My teacher] said, 'Imagine you're a stick of gum. And when you engage in sex that's like, that's like getting chewed. And then if you do that lots of times you're gonna become an old piece of gum. And who's going to want you after that?' Well that's terrible.

Nobody should ever say that. But for me, I thought, oh my gosh, I'm that chewed up piece of gum."[1]

Smart's high-profile story of being kidnapped and eventually rescued was covered by every major news media outlet in the country, but she's far from the only survivor of assault or abuse to feel this way. The things we learn—or the things we *don't* learn—in sex education stick with us for life, long after we've learned how to use Google to get the answers we need.

This is, of course, true of all sexuality education, religious and secular, but purity culture in particular has a fraught relationship with sex ed. Purity culture can only thrive in ignorance. It is based almost entirely on false claims—theological, emotional, spiritual, and yes, physical. For advocates of purity culture, robust and comprehensive sex ed for young people is a worst-case scenario. If young people are empowered with knowledge and truth about their bodies and sex, then they will see the claims of purity culture for what they are: almost laughable. Purity culture shrivels in the glaring light of day. So the only real solution if you want to try to guarantee that young people will wait until marriage to have sex is to get a vise grip on the flow of knowledge into your community and only allow in information that coheres with the worldview you've already committed to, carefully filtered through an interpretive lens that ensures that unacceptable ideas will never be entertained.

Many families and churches mired in purity culture don't offer any sex education at all. Several women have told me stories of being given hurried, last-minute advice on the eve of their weddings even though their parents had never talked to them about sex in the past. Others, like my own family, communicate the bare minimum amount of information (as late as they possibly can) regarding the mechanics of heterosexual procreation, but not much else. The only nonprocreative piece of sex ed information I can remember is that my father mentioned during The Talk™ that men like to touch women's breasts, but you shouldn't do that until you're married either.

But regardless of *how much* information is given, often the information that *is* given is misleading, incomplete, or just flat-out false. In 2013 on the *Last Week Tonight* show, John Oliver took a deep dive into the state of sexuality education in the United States and shocked his viewers by reporting that "there is no required standard for sex ed in this country; in fact, only twenty-two states mandate that kids receive it, and only thirteen require that the information presented be medically accurate."[2] As of the writing of this book, the number has jumped to twenty-four states and the District of Columbia requiring sex ed, with twenty requiring that it be medically accurate,[3] but still—that's bleak. And remember, these government regulations apply to public schools. Private schools often have loopholes that absolve them of responsibility for educating their students on issues of sexuality from a comprehensive and medically accurate viewpoint, and even public schools often allow parents to opt their children out of sex education.

This doesn't even begin to cover the regulations for homeschooling, which vary widely from state to state. In Illinois, where I grew up, there was little to no regulation of homeschooling whatsoever. I was fortunate to have one parent with postsecondary education, and though my mother had no education beyond high school, she was diligent in selecting the curriculum for me and my siblings and connecting with other homeschooling parents for resource sharing and further education. Academically, my homeschooling experience was more than adequate, and I earned straight As when I started college at the age of sixteen. But others weren't so lucky. I knew kids who were being "homeschooled" who weren't being schooled in any way whatsoever. And certainly no one checked in to make sure that we were being given accurate information about sex and our bodies. Hell, Illinois didn't even require standardized testing for homeschoolers at the time. My health textbook in eighth grade replaced what should have been the sex ed unit with a unit on "spiritual health," which taught me about such important topics as the harmful decibel levels of rock music.

As a student at Moody Bible Institute, I made a fun hobby out of taking screenshots of all the different ways I managed to set off the school's internet filters. I once got blocked for "abortion" because I was looking at a pro-life website for my ethics class. Another time, I was blocked for "pornography" for Googling "modest swimsuits." The other day I was telling this story to my fiancée, Caitlin, who got her bachelor's degree in sociology from Spring Arbor University, a small Christian liberal arts school in Michigan. Spring Arbor had internet filters similar to Moody's. Caitlin told me that once, while taking a class on gender and sexuality, she was blocked from viewing a website because it fell under the category of "sex education." "A lot of times I had to do research for my class on my phone," she said, "because I couldn't access any of the websites I needed on a computer that was connected to the school's network."

And while Spring Arbor University may have codified this rejection of sex education into its actual policies, churches and families everywhere do this every day in less formal, and less explicit, ways. But the reason for this lack of sex education is always clear. In the minds of these parents, pastors, and teachers, the government doesn't care about God's word or God's dictates that everyone remain sexually abstinent until marriage. They believe that "the world" will try to tell their young people that anything goes as long as everyone consents. "Sex education," they assume, is a slippery slope to hedonism. Conversations with my parents, youth group leaders, pastors, and professors only affirmed this line of thought. You don't need sex education if you just follow the rules.

Joshua McDowell, whom some would consider one of the fathers of the modern purity movement, said it best in his book *How to Help Your Children Say "No" to Sexual Pressure*: "When adolescents—and even younger children—learn about sex in these ways [media, sex education in schools, and friends], they're getting a biological education (which may or may not be accurate), but they're not being trained in moral responsibility. The media, their friends, and even their teachers are telling children how the body works; but they aren't telling young people how to handle their desires in a way that keeps them pure and honors God."[4] The implicit teaching is that learning how your body works and honoring God are mutually exclusive endeavors.

So what's the right way to teach children and young people about sex and sexuality according to purity culture? Purity culture takes one of two tacks when it comes to sex education: (1) don't teach anything at all, or (2) if you can't avoid teaching something, teach only information that encourages abstinence until legal, monogamous marriage between a cisgender heterosexual man and a cisgender heterosexual woman—even if you have to make things up.

Purity Culture's "Sex Education"

It's been said that Donald Trump doesn't tell lies he expects anybody else to believe. The lies he tells constantly are overt, obvious, and verifiable with a single Google search. Rather, he tells power lies. He says things he knows aren't true in defiance, daring anyone to contradict him. He knows they won't because he has the power. Trump says that he will be the one to set the parameters of reality for the people under his rule. If he says the sky is red, it's red.

Purity culture is similar. Purity culture makes a lot of claims about sex, bodies, and relationships—some based on half-truths and manipulated statistics that are rooted in reality and others just completely fabricated. But whether it's partially true or a total lie, like the diligent political fact-checkers who work day in and day out to hold the president's lies up to the microscope, fact-checking the claims of purity culture is essential. Allowing pastors, parents, and teachers to go on teaching things that are simply not factual in the name of controlling the sexuality of others cannot and should not be tolerated.

For the skeptical or not-yet-convinced, I wanted to illustrate some of these false claims. All of these came from purity culture books I already owned or articles and videos by popular teachers that are readily available online. I've included below several claims, followed by fact-checking to see just how they hold up to reality.

—

CLAIM: *Premarital sex is a sex addiction.* "Are you willing to risk an abundant life on earth and eternal life in heaven just to 'get some'? If the answer is yes—and it's not just your words but your actions on this earth that will determine that—*then an addict is exactly what you are.* You are willing to risk your eternal life for a quick fix."[5]

TRUTH: For whatever it's worth, "sex addiction" actually isn't in the Diagnostic and Statistical Manual of Mental Disorders (DSM-5). That's not to say it's never diagnosed or discussed among clinical professionals, but addictive behavior is characterized by compulsivity, like alcohol or opioid addiction.[6] Having sex outside of the context of a legal marriage is a perfectly normal thing to do and not a symptom of any addiction.

CLAIM: Condoms don't work. "Using condoms to prevent the spread of HIV is about as dangerous as putting two bullets in a six-chamber gun and playing Russian roulette."[7]

TRUTH: For people with penises or those who have sex with them, using condoms is a crucial part of preventing the spread of HIV as well as many other sexually transmitted infections. Some people also take a prevention pill called PreP. Condoms used properly and consistently are far more than 66 percent effective at preventing HIV—actually closer to 90 to 95 percent.

CLAIM: Erotic literature ruins the experience of partnered sex. "Normal sex in your marriage—the kind that requires communication, sometimes involves frustration, and doesn't always end in rapturous orgasm—will now be disappointing."[8]

TRUTH: Reading (or writing) erotic literature has no inherent correlation to sexual satisfaction with one's spouse or any other sexual partner. Anecdotally, some couples have even credited the reading or writing of erotica with improving their sex lives.

CLAIM: Failing to follow the precepts of purity culture leads to depression and suicide. "Once a teenage girl engages in sexual intercourse outside of marriage, she becomes three times more likely to commit suicide than a girl who is a virgin."[9]

TRUTH: First of all, the "study" cited above was put out by the Heritage Foundation, whose mission is "to formulate and promote conservative public policies based on the principles of free enterprise, limited government, individual freedom, traditional American values, and a strong national defense"[10]—so I would trust that study about as much as I would trust a study from the US cattle industry claiming that cheeseburgers are the latest health food. Second of all, both depression and suicide have multiple factors of causation, and studies have shown that when it comes to issues of sexuality, the presence of parental or other adult figures in a teen's life who are supportive and affirming make the biggest difference between positive and negative mental health outcomes.[11]

CLAIM: Like tape that's lost its stickiness, people who have sex with more than one person can no longer bond with others in healthy ways. "How many partners do we have before we get married on average in America? Six, yeah. So can you imagine what's gonna start to happen to the tape? It's gonna lose its bonding power."[12]

TRUTH: It's true that the hormone oxytocin, sometimes called "the love hormone," is released during sex. Oxytocin plays a powerful role in creating a sense of "connectedness"—which might be why it's also released during breastfeeding. But you don't see anyone going around telling people not to breastfeed more than one kid because they might not be able to bond as well with the second one. In reality, mutual, positive, healthy sexual relationships don't prevent anyone from bonding well with future sexual partners.

CLAIM: Life begins (or a soul is present) when a sperm cell meets an egg. "Science agrees on this point. Life begins at conception."[13]

TRUTH: Pregnancy begins when a fertilized egg implants on the wall of the uterus. This doesn't happen every time a sperm meets an egg. It's impossible to know the exact numbers, but scientists estimate that between one-third and one-half of all fertilized eggs don't make it to implantation—and therefore don't cause a person to become pregnant.[14] The fertilized eggs that don't implant on the uterine wall are reabsorbed by the body without the person ever knowing fertilization took place. And that's just referring to the scientific definition of *pregnancy*.[15] This is to say nothing of *life*, a term that is often used interchangeably with *personhood* or *soul* and that is something that science cannot quantify. Claiming scientific consensus around "when life begins" is a fantasy at best and outright deception at worst.

CLAIM: Abstinence will increase your fertility. "[God] made you to be healthy and to 'be fruitful and increase in number' (Genesis 1:22), and abstinence will greatly increase your ability to do so."[16]

TRUTH: There is no correlation between abstinence until legal marriage and fertility.

CLAIM: You can "put yourself in a situation" to be sexually abused if you're not careful. "My no didn't mean no, and I was sexually abused by a man who did the same things to me that I had read about in those [erotica] stories. But in my story, there wasn't a happy ending. Ever since then, I have carried the weight of shame and guilt from putting myself into that situation six years ago."[17]

TRUTH: The fault of abuse always lies with the person doing the abusing. No one can be blamed for "putting themselves in the situation."

—

I could keep going, but listing each and every lie touted by purity culture would be a never-ending Sisyphean task. The bulk of sexuality-related "facts" presented in popular purity culture literature are either completely made-up lies or based in some scientific evidence but have been spliced together misleadingly to support the agenda of the author and tow the purity party line.

Hordes of parents, pastors, and Christian teachers are out here telling our children blatant lies about sex, biology, bodies, and relationships in the name of "keeping them pure" and "honoring God." Some might say that while it's not good to lie, if what you tell children and young adults helps them stay pure until marriage, then the ends justify the Scotch-taped means. Others might dig in their heels and insist that these aren't lies at all—that the "world" presents only facts that justify their lascivious lifestyles and that those whose minds are truly illuminated by the Holy Spirit are able to understand how the facts support teaching mandatory abstinence until legal monogamous marriage to someone with different primary sex characteristics than you. But regardless of *why* someone might be in favor of teaching these things, the fact remains that there are dire consequences when young people go out into the world with little or inaccurate information about sex and their bodies.

When I learned that the clitoris existed and where it was located (thanks to a little Googling), I was twenty-one years old and had just graduated college. What I had assumed was the urethra was actually the clitoris. I was a veritable purity culture professional—at twenty-one, I hadn't even had my first kiss. I had sat through hours of purity-based sex education with my parents, with my youth group, and even in college classes. Never once did anybody talk about pleasure in sex, and never once did anybody tell me I was the proud owner of something called a clitoris.

My own misunderstanding was easily rectified through five minutes of research. By the time I did start having sex, I had (re)educated myself enough to be able to positively communicate using biologically accurate terms about what did and didn't feel good. But unfortunately, the problems for many purity culture graduates don't stop at simple mix-ups. And unfortunately, many of the problems that arise from insufficient or inaccurate sex education feed directly into the #ChurchToo crisis.

You Are Not Your Own

One common theme in purity-based sex education is the idea that your body does not belong solely to you. That's one of the main reasons not to have sex, actually; because you are not your own and were bought with a price (1 Corinthians 6:19b–20 NIV), you need to treat your body like something valuable you are borrowing from someone else. Depending on the community, sometimes it will be emphasized that your body actually belongs to God, and sometimes it will be emphasized that your body belongs to your future husband or wife. These emphases are different but equally harmful. Under the assumption that young people's bodies do not belong to them, they are not taught to be able to say yes or no to the type of sexual contact they would or would not like to have. Their desires are, in general, irrelevant. It doesn't matter what you want; it matters what is right. And what is right is located outside of you, in the authority of

God as revealed in the bible and mediated to you by parents, teachers, and pastors.

So when parents, teachers, pastors, and others in authority over someone (such as a boyfriend or husband in a complementarian community) are the abusers, this can put their victims in a very sticky situation. Their bodies don't belong to them, after all. They have been conditioned from their earliest memories to view their bodies as under the authority of external sources. They don't get to say yes or no to what happens to them. Sometimes, in communities with an added emphasis on bodies belonging to a future spouse, abusers will even (as mine did) promise to marry their victims in order to gain their trust and make them feel like what is happening is right. If marriage is promised, then the abuser becomes the mythical future spouse to whom the victim's body belongs. One can see how easily predators might weaponize this theology to select and groom their victims effortlessly, without having to change their existing worldview to ensnare them in their web.

Naivety Is the Best Policy

Whether it's the mechanics of pleasure or the existence of nonheterosexual sexualities (covered more in the next chapter), much of purity culture's sex education tends to assume that the less people know, the better. If we tell young people too much, they might get curious and start experimenting—and we can't have that. Teaching young people who have a clitoris that they have a body part that doesn't do anything except give pleasure might encourage them to start masturbating—or worse, make them think that they deserve to feel pleasure, even with other people. If we acknowledge the vast spectrum of human sexuality, it might put the idea in our kids' heads to be gay. If we teach them how to use condoms or tell them that there's a vaccine that can prevent certain types of human papillomavirus (HPV) as well as cervical cancer, they might take that as a license to sin and start having premarital sex!

But in reality, knowledge is power—and children and young people being empowered with the knowledge they need is a crucial part of preventing abuse or cutting it off at the root when it starts to happen. Heather Corinna, cofounder of Scarleteen, one of the most influential sexuality education websites for young people, put it this way in a 2009 op-ed for the *Guardian*:

> A child who knows they have the right to their own boundaries—even with adults—who is being sexually abused is one far more likely to know they are being abused and who will feel more empowered to tell someone what is happening so the abuse will stop. A child who knows the names of their own body parts, and that those parts are not for just anyone to touch or take, can more easily identify when and where someone shouldn't be touching them. Better still, this knowledge can help a child identify some of the initial ways boundaries may be pushed or dismissed before abuse begins so that it is prevented full-stop.[18]

Statistically speaking, ignorance does not stop anyone from having premarital sex. Occasionally it may delay the onset of sexual activity outside of marriage by a short period of time, but that is not the same thing as preventing abuse. Parents, pastors, and educators should let that one sink in. *Preventing premarital sex is not the same thing as preventing abuse.*

Convincing Is Not Consent

As I mentioned in the previous chapter, many of the cautionary tales of loss of virginity in popular purity culture literature are actually stories of coercion, sexual assault, and rape that are presented as consensual encounters where both people involved are equally at fault. Most purity-based sex education doesn't use the word *consent* or deal with the concept because there is only one kind of acceptable "consensual" sexual activity—married sex between a cisgender man and a cisgender woman. You don't need to be worried about something like consent, because before marriage, everything is off limits—and after marriage, everything is on the table.

Joshua McDowell shared this story in *How to Help Your Child Say "No" to Sexual Pressure*:

> Bryan turned to Shauna and looked at her with very serious, but loving, eyes and asked her, "Shauna, do you love me?" Shauna chuckled and said, "That's a dumb question. Of course I love you!" Bryan then said, "If you love me, you'll prove it by having sex with me. If you won't then I will no longer be able to be your boyfriend." What could Shauna do? She would never want to give up Bryan, but she knew sex before marriage was wrong. She decided she loved Bryan more and gave in. Within a week, Bryan and Shauna had broken up and neither had respect for the other. Did Shauna really love Bryan? Not really, but she thought she did. However, that fear of losing Bryan overcame her.[19]

In McDowell's narrative, this story serves as an illustration of how wrong Shauna was—how she didn't really love Bryan and how she just didn't have the conviction or inner strength not to have premarital sex with him and later regretted it. But McDowell is missing a crucial piece of the puzzle here—namely, that in this parable, *Bryan is actually a rapist.* If someone doesn't want to have sex with you but you convince them to have sex with you anyway using threats and fear, that is rape. The same goes for any other methods of convincing, from drugs and alcohol to spiritual authority.

This is an obvious example, but the principle is ubiquitous in purity culture's understanding of sexual encounters. If it's premarriage, it's a sin—simple as that. Who cares who consented and who didn't? Genitals were interacting outside of that sacred, covenantal context. Nothing else matters. And when it comes to a revelation of abuse, ultimately it's a lot tidier to say that both people were at fault for having premarital (or extramarital) sex than it is to confront the fact that someone we thought was a godly man or a good leader was actually a rapist or an abuser. This theology flattens out the very large difference between consensual sex and assault and often plays a role in blaming the victim for what happened when abuse does occur. And it's particularly insidious when this theology is cloaked in spurious "facts" and "studies" and presented to vulnerable people as real medical advice that's backed up by science and common sense as well as the bible.

—

As I was writing this chapter, I couldn't stop thinking about what Dr. Tina Schermer Sellers had told me about parents, pastors, and teachers who will only provide abstinence-only sex education to their children and students: "You've given them no knowledge. You've given them no resources, nothing to equip them to protect themselves. . . . And then you send them out into the world, and they are as naked as they can be. They cannot protect themselves. . . . It's like throwing your children to the wolves. You've just done that."

I can't help but think about myself and all the survivors of the #ChurchToo crisis who were thrown to the wolves because our parents, pastors, and teachers were more concerned about making sure we believed the right thing and didn't "ruin" our purity than they were about empowering us and making sure we had the information and education we needed to be healthy and thrive. Make no mistake about it, the choice to withhold scientifically and medically accurate sexuality education from young people and only give them the half-truths and lies that shore up the worldview you want them to have is a theological one—and it's deeply immoral. I don't believe that the people who made that choice for my generation were evil despots who wanted their children to be miserable and vulnerable to exploitation. But I do believe that evangelical Christians who are committed to purity culture show by their actions that they love their ideas about who God is and what God wants more than they love the actual people in front of them. And I do believe that there are many parents and pastors out there who, even if confronted with incontrovertible evidence that giving children comprehensive, consent-based sexuality education leads to better mental and physical health outcomes and less vulnerability to abuse, would still choose purity culture every time, because they genuinely believe it's the right thing to do.

Sometimes it feels like a whole generation of us were sacrificed on the altar of abstinence. God asked our parents and our pastors and our teachers to sacrifice us—or so they thought. And like Abraham leading his son Isaac to slaughter, they dutifully built the fire and readied the knife. But we weren't as fortunate as Isaac. There was no substitutionary ram in the thicket. There was no one to rescue us—from them, from purity culture, or from the God we learned about as we lay there.

—

My parents taught me and my siblings when we were children that according to the bible, the earth is about six thousand years old. For an assignment in homeschool co-op[20] when I was about fourteen, we counted up all the years in the genealogies in the bible in order to get the sum total of six thousand, proving once and for all that the earth is young. My mother made us fast forward through the first two minutes of every *The Land before Time* dinosaur cartoon so that we wouldn't hear the speech in the introduction about the world being "millions of years" old. The idea of evolution, we were taught, was a worldwide conspiracy on the part of the government, school teachers, and other non-Christians because they didn't recognize the authority of our Scripture and didn't want to obey God. We even made a family pilgrimage to the Creation Museum in Kentucky, which presents information only from a young-earth creationist viewpoint.

The textbooks we read and the moms teaching us at co-op undertook some truly Olympian gymnastics to explain why all the scientific evidence makes it look like the earth is so much older than six thousand years. It could be explained by the worldwide flood of Genesis! It could be flash petrification of wood! But my favorite excuse was this one: maybe God made everything look old and put dinosaur bones where we found them in order to test our faith and see if we really believed the bible. That's right: maybe the bulk of scientific evidence suggesting one thing is really evidence that its opposite is true.

This maneuver is so widespread in conservative Christianity that Christians are often desensitized to the fact that they're even pulling it. The "sex education" provided within purity culture is merely one example. The bulk of all the evidence that we have—the academic studies, the words of sex educators and therapists and doctors, and so, so much anecdotal evidence—suggests that the healthiest outcomes happen when children and young people are given age-appropriate, comprehensive, consent-based sexuality education and are empowered to take charge of their bodies and learn to say yes and no to what they do and don't want. Purity culture proponents claim that all of that information has been put there to test us. If we really believed the bible, we would reject the false flags of science and experience and dig our heels into teaching, and living, purity culture.

This is not good enough for me. It is not good enough for the many survivors of the #ChurchToo epidemic who were thrown to the wolves. And it should not be good enough for you either. Adherence to a belief system should never require us to check our brains at the door or consign ourselves or others to lives of purposeful ignorance and needless suffering. It may be scary for you to think about what children and young people will build with the tools we give them. So be it. It is not as scary as another generation of young people primed for abuse and dysfunction by a system that does not care about them and will not help them rebuild in its aftermath.

6

MALE AND FEMALE HE CREATED THEM

So God created humankind in his image, in the image of God he created them; male and female he created them. God blessed them, and God said to them, "Be fruitful and multiply, and fill the earth and subdue it."

—Genesis 1:27–28a

If the last three years since the launch of #ChurchToo have taught me anything, it's that this is the chapter where I start to lose people in droves. When I say that there's a problem with sexualized violence in Christian communities, people are tracking with me. When I go further and say that purity culture is bad and is a contributing factor to cultures of abuse, people usually stay on board, albeit sometimes by redefining *purity culture* as "being mean about abstinence"—but hey, I'm always thankful when people keep listening. But when I go one step further and suggest that to truly dismantle a culture of abuse, you have to not only tolerate but accept, affirm, and celebrate LGBTQ persons and their relationships in all the myriad forms they take, suddenly nobody wants to touch me with a ten-foot pole.

For months in late 2017 and early 2018, most Christian publications ignored the existence of #ChurchToo, even as it went viral on mainstream media news sites. Ironically, "the world" gave the movement a better reception than the church did. Eventually, articles began to pop up on websites like the Gospel Coalition and *Christianity Today* referencing "Evangelicalism's #MeToo Moment," but they were careful never to actually name "#ChurchToo." It was like Christian media outlets were channeling that Mariah Carey gif whenever the topic of #ChurchToo came up: "I can't read suddenly. I don't know." *sunglasses*

But we all knew why. #ChurchToo began when a queer woman came forward about her abuse in the evangelical church. A queer woman who wasn't sorry for being queer, who wasn't running back to the evangelical church with her tail between her legs promising to be celibate or go to conversion therapy if only they'd accept her. A queer woman who was well educated in the finer points of evangelical apologetics and held a degree from one of their most respected institutions of higher learning. A queer woman who had nothing left to lose.

I was basically the worst nightmare of the evangelical Christian purity industrial complex. And they wanted nothing to do with me.

Shortly after #ChurchToo launched, a woman on Twitter claiming to be an expert on abuse and a "certified trauma therapist" was even kind enough to inform me that LGBTQ identities are actually a completely separate issue from patriarchy and sexual abuse and that if I didn't stop advocating for LGBTQ folks alongside #ChurchToo work, I was going to traumatize #ChurchToo survivors who "did not agree with LGBTQ identities." She even went as far as saying that highlighting LGBTQ survivors of #ChurchToo violence was "dangerous" and "distracting" and that I was changing the meaning of #ChurchToo.

For reasons I cannot comprehend, it is still considered appropriate and polite in many Christian communities to "disagree" with LGBTQ identities. Often Christians share their "disagreement" with LGBTQ identities without hesitation or shame on social media or in conversation, and others are expected to respect those beliefs as if they were merely a legitimate difference of opinion and not either an indication of extreme ignorance or a failure of moral reasoning. Like most queer people with religious affiliations, I've been the recipient of the classic "We love you but we don't agree with your lesbian lifestyle" line. I was expected to just accept this statement as normal and appropriate and move on to talking about soccer games and surgeries as if nothing had happened.

In some churches, a nonaffirming stance toward LGBTQ persons and relationships has even become a litmus test of true Christianity. Those who affirm LGBTQ identities or show any human softness toward the plight of LGBTQ persons in the church are seen as having compromised their Christianity and caved in to "the world" or as having less skill in interpreting the bible. This way of thinking is pervasive in Christian churches, schools, and other faith communities in the United States, and it is incredibly dangerous. Theology that rejects the personhood, value, and created goodness of LGBTQ people and relationships is a crucial building block of the culture of sexualized violence that created #ChurchToo. Many wish to deny this fact because it means that they will have to rethink their sexual ethics and fling wide the door to welcome in those they had previously cast out, but fear of having to change your mind is not a good enough reason to avoid looking the facts squarely in the face. There is a direct line between the homophobia that is so often justified using the bible and the trauma—and retraumatization—of survivors of sexualized violence in the church.

—

Many queer folks have always known that they were queer. From a very early age, they describe having had a strong sense of their sexual orientation or gender identity and a sense that they were different from those around them. Lady Gaga summed up this experience in her song "Born This Way" when she sang, "I'm beautiful in my way / cause God makes no mistakes / I'm on the right track, baby / I was born this way."

I, on the other hand, definitely did not "always know," and the "Born This Way" narrative does not ring true to my lived experience. I've always been a little jealous of those for whom it does, because my own experience has always been somewhat perplexing to me. In classic lesbian fashion, I was really good at purity culture—I got through high school and all of undergrad without a single kiss on the lips. My worst purity culture failure was some awkward flip-phone sexting with my high school boyfriend and some brief, ill-fated cuddling in Moody Makeout Park (the park near school where everyone went to make out; not its real name; yes, students really called it that; and no, I did not do any actual "making out" in it).

I "dated" men my whole life but never had sex until my twenties. And to be honest, abstinence wasn't particularly hard. When I commit to something, I tend to turn into somewhat of a discipline robot. By the time I started getting into relationships as an adult, I had shut off all connections to my own sexuality. I had fully internalized the message given to me by my family and my church that what I wanted was irrelevant at best and deadly at worst. The idea to be interested in or date women would never have occurred to me during that time because my decisions were based not on desire or curiosity but rather on what was acceptable based on the narrow interpretation of Scripture I had been taught. It's not so much that I was stuffing any desires down consciously; it was more that the connection between my body and my mind had been severed long before I ever had my first boyfriend or my first kiss. Purity culture created and then reinforced that disconnect, making me feel like I was a better person than my friends for being able to resist temptation so valiantly. But the truth is, I simply didn't know what I wanted because I'd never been given the freedom to consider my own desires.

So I dated men. And eventually, I married one. In almost every way, he was my first. And I'm sure if he had been an asshole or a terrible lover, I would have understood my predicament much more quickly, but he was neither. I'd been married for over a year when the lightbulb in my head finally turned on and I realized that I wasn't straight.

When I told my #ChurchToo story on Twitter a year and a half after that realization, I was still married and identifying as bisexual. But in the months that followed, it became clear that bisexuality may have been my chosen identification because I was already married to a man, but it was not actually the truth about me. Over time, the label became a door that I hid behind because I was terrified to know what was on the other side and at the same time desperately desired it.

In the years that followed, I came out as gay and got a divorce, and I am still learning what it means to live in my true identity as a queer woman. But I share all of this to say, first and foremost, that I am unapologetically a queer woman, and I am unable to take off my queerness like a jacket and set it aside while I do the work of #ChurchToo in order to make people more comfortable with me or the work. My identity as a gay woman and my commitment to justice for all LGBTQ persons will always inform the work I do around sexualized violence in the church.

I also share all of this to say that I have had a front-row seat to the tragic spectacle of the way the church treats LGBTQ persons, and it has negatively affected my life personally. I know that there are no alternate timelines and there is no way to go back and find out "what if?"—but I often wish that I had grown up in a home where healthy human sexuality and comprehensive sex ed were modeled and taught. I wish I had grown up in a home where it would have been OK and safe for me, as a young girl, to feel my feelings and be aware of my desires and know that no one would punish me or condemn me to hell for them. I think of the people I could have avoided hurting if I had known myself better and sooner, and it makes me weep.

So many of us have these weird, complicated, heartbreaking stories—more than you can possibly imagine. We are all casualties of a purity culture that says there is only one right way to have a body and only one right way to love. "Love the sinner, hate the sin" pretends that there is a way to reject LGBTQ persons and relationships while not contributing to their oppression and death. This is a dangerous fiction.

Dietrich Bonhoeffer, otherwise known as every evangelical's favorite guy to misinterpret, was a twentieth-century pastor, writer, and public theologian who got himself embroiled in an assassination plot to kill Adolf Hitler and was eventually hanged by the Nazis for it in 1945. I think often of Bonhoeffer's "wheel of injustice": he famously said, "We are not to simply bandage the wounds of victims beneath the wheels of injustice, we are to drive a spoke into the wheel itself." I imagine the crisis of #ChurchToo as that wheel, being connected by various wires and chains and gears, all of which work together to make the wheel functional. Homophobia, or what some call "nonaffirming" theology, is one of the gears—even though so many people try to deny this fact. You will see a lot of people pretending like #ChurchToo is merely an issue of individual bad men abusing women and has nothing to do with our theologies of sexuality. You will see people who claim that they care well for survivors of church sexual abuse turn around and perpetuate the dangerous myths and lies about LGBTQ sexualities that have helped create such a sexually dysfunctional culture in their churches in the first place. As the apostle Paul (or, more likely according to biblical scholars, a person writing as the apostle Paul) once said, "The time is coming when people will not put up with sound doctrine, but having itching ears, they will accumulate for themselves teachers to suit their own desires, and will turn away from listening to the truth and wander away to myths" (2 Timothy 4:3–4).

Homophobia Is Sexualized Violence

In order to understand the role that nonaffirming theology or homophobia plays in the crisis of #ChurchToo, it is first necessary to understand homophobia as sexualized violence. To be clear, what I am saying is that theology that teaches that heterosexuality is the only sexual orientation acceptable to God—and that all LGBTQ persons must either seek to change their sexuality via therapy/prayer or else remain permanently celibate if they are unsuccessful—is violence.

"But what about—"

No. Your theology is not special. You have not found the one magical theology that rejects LGBTQ persons and relationships but isn't violence. And yes, I have to include "and relationships." Some people will claim to be affirming of LGBTQ *persons* as long as they don't have a sexual or romantic relationship. That's not affirming, and that's still violence.

"So I just have to agree with my gay kid/brother/sister/ coworker's lifestyle or I'm a bigot?"

Kind of. What I'm saying is that the identities and relationships of LGBTQ persons *cannot be agreed with or disagreed with, because existence is not a matter of opinion.* If I asked you if you agree that the sky is blue or water is wet, wouldn't you look at me as if I asked a nonsense question? Exactly.

Far from being a matter of hermeneutics or a mere difference in opinion, nonaffirming theology is full-blown sexualized violence. Nonaffirming theology is homophobia, and homophobia heaps violence on LGBTQ people as well as their families, friends, and church communities. "Whenever an individual fails to deal with their sexuality in a healthy manner," liberation theologian Miguel A. De La Torre teaches, "it will manifest itself in destructive ways, not just for the individuals, but also the overall community."[1] Except that most of the time, LGBTQ persons living in evangelical Christian communities are not simply "failing" to deal with their sexuality in a healthy way but rather are *forbidden* from doing so.

When the things you must do to be healthy are the very things you are forbidden from doing or you put yourself in danger of excommunication and hellfire, you are at serious risk of harm. It's estimated that 40 percent of the total population of homeless youth is LGBTQ, a wild overrepresentation.[2] When I volunteered on the streets of Boystown during my time at Moody, I saw that often these homeless youth came from conservative religious environments that did not recognize LGBTQ sexualities as valid, and many were kicked out of their parents' homes as a result of coming out.

Multiple studies have shown that LGBTQ individuals have higher rates of depression, anxiety, self-harm, and suicide attempts. One study in particular showed that lesbian and bisexual young women had significantly higher rates of mental health problems than their heterosexual peers, with bisexual young women having higher rates of suicide than either heterosexual women or lesbians. Likewise, in the same study, gay and bisexual young men scored significantly higher than heterosexual men when it came to various mental health issues.[3]

If one were unapologetic in their bigotry and unwilling to dig deeper, one might conclude from these studies and anecdotes that there is something about being LGBTQ in itself that leads to negative mental health outcomes. One might even use this as "proof" that LGBTQ identities and relationships are sinful. Tim LaHaye of Left Behind fame certainly did. His book *The Unhappy Gays: What Everyone Should Know about Homosexuality*, first published in 1978, is admittedly quite dated, and I doubt that a book like it would be greenlit today by even the most conservative publishers. But it encapsulates the idea that the suffering of LGBTQ persons has to do with who they *are* and not what has been done to them: "There is no question in my mind that homosexuals experience more rejection than anyone else on earth—by their parents, loved ones, God, society, and, tragically, even by homosexuals themselves. Because homosexuals are so selfish, many reject and run roughshod over the feelings of their not-so-gay friends. Although there is no way of positively verifying it, I can believe the suggestion that homosexuals account for 50 percent of America's suicides. . . . The tremendous rejection homosexuals experience inevitably brings them to depression at a rate many times higher than that of the straight community."[4]

Now, aside from LaHaye's tenuous grasp on the concept of statistics, it's utterly staggering that someone can acknowledge the high rate of depression and suicide among the LGBTQ community and further acknowledge its origination in the rejection of family and society and still manage to blame LGBTQ people. But even though *The Unhappy Gays* is an exaggerated and, at times, almost comically bad take on LGBTQ issues in America, the ideas it contains have not gone away in the intervening four decades since its publication. They've simply been filtered, turned into a more palatable homophobia that appeals to silence rather than outright rejection.

The problem with believing that depression, anxiety, and other mental health struggles are just part and parcel of what it means to be LGBTQ is that the data doesn't hold up.

LGBTQ young people in particular are vulnerable to these struggles—but studies have shown that they don't have to be: "LGBTQ youth who report having at least one accepting adult were 40% less likely to report a suicide attempt in the past year."[5] Not only that, but "LGBTQ children with unaffirming parents are at higher risk for negative physical and mental health issues, including depression, anxiety, sexual risk behaviors, substance use, suicidal thinking, and more."[6] However, the presence of supportive parents has been shown to work as a protective factor against all of the above. Far from being inherent traits, mental health struggles, substance use, risky sexual behaviors, and more are all logical consequences of theology that rejects LGBTQ identities and relationships—which is why homophobia is violence: it literally leads to death. But these deadly consequences can be prevented and in some cases even reversed. If Christian parents are invested in their LGBTQ children living long, happy, and healthy lives, literally all they have to do is accept and support them without trying to make them change. In other words, as Dr. Tina Schermer Sellers told me, parents must make themselves "resilient enough to hear their truth." Statistically speaking, it really is that simple.

Theology that rejects the created goodness of LGBTQ persons and fails to uphold their relationships as valid is a violence that has, as Hilary and Stephanie from Into Account defined it, "both a sexual form of expression and a sexual logic." And I am struck by the number of conservative Christians who make a big show about being "against sexual violence" but fail to see their theology of LGBTQ persons as a manifestation of that very violence they so loudly protest. It is intellectually dishonest to only oppose some sexualized violences and not others, especially when there is so much irrefutable evidence that the shame the church heaps on LGBTQ individuals is quite literally killing them.

But it's not just a matter of intellectual dishonesty. Homophobia should be opposed not just because it is inconsistent and deadly but also because it plays a critical role in building the sexually dysfunctional culture that created #ChurchToo. Justice and affirmation for LGBTQ persons in and out of the church are intimately connected to #ChurchToo, because the rot of #ChurchToo can only grow in a dark, damp environment where healthy human sexuality is strangled and dies out and the thorny weeds of sexual violence and abuse of power are the only things that can survive.

Homophobic theology intersects with #ChurchToo in two main ways: before and after. Before abuse, homophobic theology labors alongside modesty rules, compulsory abstinence, ignorance of consent, and poor sex education to construct the bedrock of the #ChurchToo crisis. Excluding LGBTQ relationships is just one arm of purity culture, which excludes all sexual relationships outside of one man and one woman in a legal, monogamous marriage for life. Nonaffirming theology creates a sexually toxic environment characterized by shame and secrecy, which is an environment ripe for abuse. A church in which normal, healthy human sexuality (including LGBTQ sexuality) is pathologized and all sexual expression is funneled into one singular, narrow avenue is a church that abusive people will be attracted to. It is also a church in which congregants will be formed and discipled to believe that extreme sexual dysfunction and toxicity is good, healthy, and even holy or required of them by God.

After abuse, homophobic theology can be extremely retraumatizing. LGBTQ survivors may be reticent to come forward out of fear of being outed and forced into conversion therapy or blamed for what happened to them. Queer people in general are hypersexualized regardless of their actual level of sexual activity, and this too often shows up in church and other Christian contexts and leads to victim-blaming. It's the same reason heterosexual couples on Christian college campuses are prohibited from having premarital sex but allowed small displays of affection like holding hands and sharing short hugs—but if same-sex couples were to hold hands while walking through these campuses, they would risk being expelled. There is an automatic assumption of hypersexuality for LGBTQ persons because being queer is viewed as a choice—a choice they could unmake if they just had enough self-control. If they could control their sexuality, they wouldn't be gay, so the logic goes. So if they're out of control sexually, why would anyone believe them when they say they were assaulted or abused?

Kenny and Michael

"I think a lot about the toxic masculinity in the youth group," Michael said over Skype, half to me and half to his childhood friend Kenny, whose face appeared in a little box on my computer screen next to Michael's. "It wasn't even just boys making jokes quietly to themselves. It was from the stage. They were always saying things like 'Women, get back in the kitchen!' and like . . ." Michael trailed off. "Kenny, what were some of the other ones?"

"'Feminazi' was the one I remember all the time," Kenny said. "Do you remember what examples they gave of 'feminazi' stuff?" he asked Michael.

Michael exhaled sharply. "It was always just whenever a girl had an opinion," he said.

Kenny rubbed his temples. "Yeah. You're right, dude," he said. "You're absolutely right."

Kenny and Michael were both sexually abused by the same man in the same Southern Baptist youth group in the 1990s, along with Michael's brother Brooks. Kenny is straight, Michael is gay, and they each reacted differently to their abuse—particularly when it came to their fears.

Kenny told me that even though he was abused by a man, fear of church members or friends thinking he was gay or making assumptions about his sexuality never really entered his mind. But for Michael, it was a much different story: "I was a closeted teenager, and I didn't want to be a part of the coming-forward process. I thought I would be outed. And being a member of a Southern Baptist Church in the '90s wasn't really a pleasant thing for a closeted gay kid. So I just avoided it."

Kenny and Brooks pressed on and attempted to come forward about their abuse, but the church they were attending swept the abuse under the rug and never made a report. For his part, Kenny completely understood why Michael didn't want to come forward: "He knew that because he was gay, people were going to say that he wanted it to happen. And his fears weren't unfounded because that's exactly what people said to me about him later."

Kenny, Michael, and Brooks all came forward about their abuse again as adults—and this time, they went public. This time, they expressed anger not only at their abuser and the church but also at the broader Christian culture that created, enabled, and sustained their abuser.

"Think about the context and culture in which our abuse happened," Michael said. "Especially for someone who's closeted, it was a gut-punch. I freaked out. I didn't want to be mocked. Othered."

"Everything that our youth group did was directed toward men," Kenny added. He told me a story about how during their time in youth group, the youth pastor would do a WWF wrestling-themed Wednesday-night service that was more of a performance than anything else. "The girls were just supposed to laugh. Everything was about dominance and maleness. And that was normal. That's just the lane that we lived in."

"During this whole period," Michael said, "I was still hoping and praying that the god I still believed in would change me. I knew I was gay, but I was still hoping, and I would literally pray that God would just take it away. Before the abuse, but especially after the abuse." The god of evangelicalism never answered Michael's prayers, and he identifies as an agnostic now.

I asked Kenny and Michael what role they think non-affirming theology plays in the #ChurchToo crisis. "I see homophobia as an extension of misogyny," Michael answered. "So the toxic culture in our church, the toxic masculinity in our church, and all of the theology of purity and complementarianism—all of that is grounded in misogyny. So is homophobia."

"I think that purity culture and the way that the American evangelical church teaches about sexuality as a whole—for LGBTQ kids but also for straight kids—is so attractive to abusers," Kenny said. "All these things that they are doing to abuse people are actually taught in the church, and they just call it 'God's design for sex' or 'God's plan for your life.' So I think #ChurchToo is just a by-product of these toxic teachings on sexuality. Then add on top of that the fact that there are kids who are trying to find themselves and understand their sexuality, who aren't willing to speak about it because they're not ready to and because they don't understand themselves. Which is perfectly natural!" Kenny sighed. "But the problem is that the demonization of homosexuality means that there's zero opportunity for these kids who are trying to figure out who they are. There is no safe place for them." I knew that feeling of having no safe place all too well.

My final question for Kenny and Michael was about what they felt was missing from the #ChurchToo conversation. One of the most frustrating things to me about #Church-Too has been watching conservative and moderate Christians attempt to make the narrative about individual bad heterosexual men doing bad things to individual heterosexual women, and if we could just create a better reporting policy and get good men to follow it, then all the problems would be solved. The problem of #ChurchToo is so much bigger and broader and more demanding than that, not the least of which is because that narrative fails to account for male and same-sex survivors of sexual abuse in the church.

"There has been a hijacking of the #ChurchToo conversation," Kenny said, the disdain in his voice palpable. "To me, that's what's missing. There are people who are voices in the #ChurchToo movement who are not willing to have that conversation about affirming theology. The narrative has shifted to what churches must do to stop abuse instead of asking how the fuck we got here in the first place."

"It makes me so angry!" I interrupted, breaking my interviewer persona for a moment. "Like, I am gay," I said, "and I started #ChurchToo. So you don't get to opt out of the conversation about LGBTQ people. You don't get to. I won't let you. My existence won't let you."

Kenny nodded. "Abuse is just what happens because of what the church has done over the years," he said. "Because of the theology, because of the homophobia, the toxic masculinity. That is what happens. So we shouldn't be surprised by the abuse."

He's right; we shouldn't be surprised to find a culture of abuse in nonaffirming communities. I, for one, have never been surprised. To me, the most surprising thing about #ChurchToo has always been that people are actually paying attention.

—

The sexualized violence of nonaffirming theology is an enormous gear on the wheel of injustice that is #ChurchToo—regardless of whether certain well-known figures talking about sexual abuse in the church today want to acknowledge it. While LGBTQ individuals and relationships are rejected, repressed, and shuffled off to therapists' offices to be "changed," sexual abuse will still thrive in churches.

But whether it affects survivors before or after abuse, the consequences of homophobic theology in the church spread far and wide. It is not an issue that Christians can afford to "pass" or be silent on, especially not when it comes to #ChurchToo. I do not believe, in the words of the great civil rights leader Fannie Lou Hamer, that anyone can be truly free until everyone is. Straight and gay and lesbian and bisexual and transgender and queer survivors and survivors of all sexualities and genders and gender identities rise and fall together. Our justice is bound up in one another's justice. And I refuse to allow myself to be used as a pawn in the contest where those with power divide between the sheep and the goats, the "good" survivors and the "bad" survivors. The survivors whose existence we acknowledge and the ones whose existence we ignore. The survivors we invite to speak at our conferences and the ones we cross our fingers and hope nobody finds out about because they challenge our sexual hierarchy. There is too much work to do to play that game.

—

A couple of months before I signed on the dotted line to write a book about #ChurchToo, I sat with Kenny in a public park in Memphis, Tennessee, on a hot July afternoon. He met me with his camera, as we planned to record a little impromptu video about #ChurchToo and how my perspective on the movement had changed in the year and a half since its launch.

I knew what we were planning on talking about in the video, but one of the questions Kenny asked me caught me by surprise. He asked me about how my personal life had changed since #ChurchToo. It'd be easier to list the ways my personal life *hadn't* changed since #ChurchToo, I thought wryly. But I started to answer. "The wild part is that everything that's happened since the beginning of #ChurchToo has coincided with a lot of really intense and painful personal growth for me," I said, "that is in many ways very unrelated to #ChurchToo and in many ways very intimately related to it. When, um . . ." I petered off.

After a long pause, I started again: "Maybe it is about #ChurchToo. Because when you garner the courage to be honest with yourself about one thing, it kind of empowers you to be honest with yourself about a lot of things. It empowers you to make big changes in other parts of your life. . . . Somehow, ripping the scab off of this wound that I had for so many years made me sort of fearless."

When #ChurchToo began, I was making a desperate, well-meaning attempt to live as a fraction of my true self.

#ChurchToo was a big part of giving me the confidence I needed to live in my full identity as a gay woman and embrace all the parts of me for what they are. I started to realize that justice for me meant being honest about who I was and what my body needed and who I was created to be. Fighting for everyone's liberation made me realize that I needed to fight for mine too, even if it meant making big changes and losing the dreams I had about my future.

#ChurchToo should never, ever, ever be used as a reason to keep someone in the closet. It should never be used to make someone feel like their sexuality or their desires have to fit into one specific mold or they won't be accepted by people or by God. When those who deny LGBTQ people the relationships and basic civil rights they deserve use #ChurchToo as a rallying cry and claim they care about justice for marginalized people, they bely the very heart and soul of #ChurchToo as a movement.

I like to imagine #ChurchToo as a trampoline, launching people toward health and wholeness and, most importantly, themselves. That's what it did for me. In beautiful, messy, complicated, perfect ways that I could not have imagined. And that's the thing about a trampoline. At a certain point, you're not in control. You're not 100 percent certain how high you will fly or where you will land. Your responsibility is to jump. Do your best. Hope your feet make contact when you land. And know that if you fall, you can get up and try again.

7

AS LONG AS HE LIVES

The last significant amount of time I spent alone with my parents was in the fall of 2014. I was twenty-three years old and engaged to be married at the time, but my soon-to-be husband was still living two time zones away, so I took this particular trip home solo. It was . . . not great. Without the buffer of my shiny new fiancé, I was exposed to the hurricane-force winds of my family's theological opinions and disdain for my work around faith and sexuality, and as hard as I tried to hold my boundaries and tell myself the cruel things they said didn't matter, I still ended up sobbing on the floor of my childhood bedroom in a panic attack my last night there. By the time I got in the car for them to drive me back to Nashville, I had already decided I was never going home alone again. I never did.

I was comatose in the back seat during the seven-hour drive, but my parents tried to make small talk nonetheless.

After some time, the conversation turned to a close friend of mine they had met who was in the beginning stages of a divorce from a cold and brutal man. She was miserable, and at times she had expressed feeling like death was a better solution than failing her family, her community, and her faith by getting divorced. She said she felt like her life was no longer of value because she didn't live up to the expectations everyone had of her. Eventually she did work up the courage to initiate a separation from her husband, and she had just moved back into her parents' house temporarily.

I relayed that information to my parents from the back seat as briefly and woodenly as I could, leaving out the details and hoping they would just accept it and move on. I was not so lucky. "You know," my father said, "if you support her in this divorce, you're supporting her in sin. The bible clearly says the only reasons you can get divorced are infidelity and abuse." I had nothing left inside of me, so I had no strength to stop myself from responding honestly. I thought about all the unspeakably mean and heartless things my friend's husband had done and said to her and about the extreme mental anguish she had been through trying to choose between her well-being and the theology that ensured her acceptance by her community. I lost it.

"What's abuse?" I spat out. "Is it only abuse if he hits her? If he leaves a bruise?" My words hung in the air between us like a thick fog.

Silence. There was no answer. They had none.

A few days after I got back to Nashville, I received a frantic late-night phone call from my friend. She was sobbing, hyperventilating. After several minutes of trying to catch her breath, she was finally able to let me know that in a last-ditch attempt to get her back, her soon-to-be ex-husband had outed her as bisexual, and her parents had kicked her out of the house. She didn't know where she was going to sleep that night.

But he didn't hit her, right? There was no bruise. So everything's fine. She would still be sinning if she left him. The bible tells us so.

One of the primary pillars of ethical nonmonogamy[1] is that no relationship is more important than the health and well-being of the people in it.[2] This is a principle that I think should be applied to all relationships, including monogamous romantic relationships, and even friendships and family relationships. The preservation of the institution of a relationship cannot be prioritized over the actual people that make it up. But purity culture teaches the opposite. Purity culture teaches that preserving a marriage relationship, once it has been created, is the highest priority for Christians. Longevity is virtually equated with success and the ending of a relationship with failure. No matter what happens, you must protect the marriage.

Sometimes, even when the "biblical criteria" for divorce *are* met,[3] the marriage is still deemed more important. The most infamous example of this kind of teaching is a video of neo-Calvinist preacher and author John Piper in which he instructs abused wives that if the abuse they are subjected to doesn't require them to sin but "simply hurts them," they should "endure verbal abuse for a season" and "endure perhaps being smacked one night" and then "seek help from the church."[4] Another crystal-clear example is from the Village Church in Dallas, Texas, which has been connected to numerous instances of sexual abuse in recent years and is led by celebrity pastor Matt Chandler. In 2015, it was revealed that when one of their overseas missionaries was found in possession of child pornography, the Village Church placed *the missionary's wife* under church discipline for beginning annulment proceedings without submitting to church marital counseling first.[5]

The trouble is, a relationship that's nearly impossible to get out of is a relationship that's ripe for abuse—especially when, as is often the case in conservative Christian communities, that relationship is characterized by strict traditional gender roles in which each partner is expected to play a certain character and any failure in that performance may result in community censure. As much as we may like to imagine marriage as a safe haven from the harsh winds of the outside world and a place of rest and renewal for each partner, it isn't always like that. And while most of the #ChurchToo stories that have made national news have been about pastors who abused their congregants, we have to reckon with the fact that stories of abuse that take place within marriages formed by purity culture are #ChurchToo stories too. In fact, I would wager that there are far more victims to be found in marriages than in churches. When one partner in a marriage has been told that their will, desires, and pleasure reign supreme over the other's by virtue of the genitals they were born with—and that this arrangement is divinely decreed by God—is it any wonder that domestic violence, rape, and sexual coercion or manipulation often result? When this abuse occurs in Christian environments, it is always a casualty of purity culture.

In purity culture, marriage is the ultimate goal of human life and the ultimate state of being. Purity culture proponents may pay lip service to the idea that single life is also valuable (especially if they are trying to convince a gay person to be celibate), but when you look at the direction in which the vast majority of programming, writing, and financial resources in the evangelical church are aimed, it couldn't be clearer: marriage is king.

But in purity culture, there's only one kind of marriage—marriage between one cisgender heterosexual man and one cisgender heterosexual woman. And in purity culture, sexuality education is severely limited, and premarital knowledge or experience of sex is strictly prohibited. Women are taught that their role is to be the gatekeepers of men's sexual purity, whereas men are taught that their role is to be the leaders of their homes, their churches, and broader society.

What could go wrong?

Megan

As I was in the process of writing this book, a woman, whom I'll call Megan,[6] reached out to me to tell me her #Church-Too story. After growing up in purity culture and promising to save her first kiss for her wedding day, Megan met and married her husband within eighteen months while attending a seminary affiliated with the Southern Baptist Church. Her abuse began on the second date.

She told me via email, "[After watching a movie at his apartment,] he leaned in to kiss me and I turned my head and said, 'That's something I'm not ready for.' He then grabbed my face, turned my head, and kissed me. I remember getting into my car and calling my father and crying that he had 'stolen my first kiss' but without a full understanding of what happened. It was met with a well-intentioned but damaging 'he just couldn't help himself.'" Things only got much, much worse from there.

In the days and weeks leading up to their wedding, Megan's fiancé often pressured her to perform sexual acts on him, and when she refused, he assaulted her. Several times during their engagement, he pinned her to the floor of his room and dry humped her until he ejaculated. The night before their wedding, he forced her to give him a hand-job despite her pleas because he said she needed to "prove she really loved him."

"I had never been taught about consent and coercion," Megan said, "so I did not realize the full extent of what was happening when we were dating and engaged. All I knew was that I felt gross and dirty and hated myself after things happened. But based on what I had been taught, that was simply 'conviction' or 'guilt' because of the sin I was engaged in."

Eventually, Megan and her fiancé did get married. Despite the numerous assaults during their dating relationship and engagement, Megan had still never had penetrative sex when they got married. "He raped me on our wedding night, rolled over, and fell asleep," she told me. They were married for three years, and during the course of those three years, Megan said she remembers one consensual sexual encounter between them. When she tried to initiate sex (at the advice of a pastor who told her that a godly wife "does not have to be forced to do anything but instead submits to her husband"), she was rejected every time. The only way her husband would make sexual contact with her during those three years was if he was raping her.

For the first half of their marriage, Megan and her husband were both still in seminary: "The seminary provided our housing, insurance, income, and education. If I left him or made his abuse known, I would have been punished by being removed from housing, fired from my job, denied health insurance, and kicked out of my master's program." It may sound hard to believe for those unfamiliar with the policies of conservative Christian schools and seminaries, but usually if you get divorced in the middle of a program, you are required to drop out, take at least a year off, and then reapply, hoping you'll be let back in if it is determined that the reason for your divorce was "biblical" and you are sufficiently repentant. So she stayed.

But a year and a half after graduating from seminary, Megan finally thought she had a biblical reason that would satisfy her Christian friends and church community. A few months shy of their third wedding anniversary, her husband confessed to her that he was "addicted to pornography." Because many evangelicals define looking at pornography as one of the worst sins a man can commit, with many teachers equating it to outright cheating or infidelity, Megan thought her community would support her in her decision to leave the marriage: "Turns out, support wasn't really a thing for the most part. I got kicked out of the church. Technically, I was placed into the process of church discipline, and I made the choice to leave instead of 'repent' and return to the marriage. I had to quit the job I had at the time. Partially because I was afraid he'd show up someday. . . . He stalked me for at least a year after the divorce finalized."

At the time we talked, it had been three years since Megan left. Her ex-husband was never able to admit that he raped her repeatedly, and the biblical "counselors"[7] they saw only served to confirm his existing worldview in which Megan was the disobedient, unsubmissive wife and he was the one who was truly being wronged. In addition to losing her church in the divorce, Megan lost many of her best friends, who could not look past their conservative theology in order to support their friend in leaving her abusive marriage. She's made new friends since then, has found a new community, and is even training to be a licensed therapist herself. But the toll that purity culture has taken on her life weighs heavily on her each and every day.

"[My abuse] was wholly and completely because of purity culture. There is no other way around it," she said. "I think the crucial pieces were the lack of teaching about consent, the emphasis on women getting married, and the lack of proper understanding of abuse. Also, [the teaching] that my worth as a female existed in my sexual purity." Add to those theological teachings an emphasis on the permanence of the marriage relationship and prohibitions against ending it even for extreme reasons and Christian marriage can become a perfect storm of toxicity and violence if one partner is an abuser. Sadly, rather than acting as a protectant, Christian teachings often *reward* the abusing partner and *prolong* the amount of time an abuser has access to their victim. And churches, which ideally would be places the abused could go to be safe and cared for, are all too often on the front lines fighting for the perpetrators.

When stories about domestic and sexual violence among churchgoing Christians are presented, many conservative Christians respond that domestic violence is obviously a tragedy, but you can't blame the church for the fact that a man chose to abuse his wife. There are bad people who do bad things in the world, after all! And abuse is perpetrated in plenty of non-Christian marriages too. So why connect this to #ChurchToo?

I'm connecting this to #ChurchToo because studies have shown the connection to be rock solid. As it turns out, acceptance of certain ideas about sex and gender roles is deeply, deeply tied to one's theology—and statistically speaking, very dangerous to the vulnerable people around them.

—

A 2018 academic study explored the intersection of particular Calvinist theological beliefs and the acceptance of what is known as *domestic violence myths* (DVMs) or *interpersonal violence myths* (IPVMs).[8] Domestic and interpersonal violence myths abound in American society, and in practice they may sound like the following:

"Well, she provoked him."
"What happens in their marriage is between the two of them. It's nobody else's business."
"He just punched a hole in the wall. It wasn't that serious."
"Why doesn't she just leave? I would."
"That would never happen to a man. He must be lying."
"She's probably just making it all up to get revenge."
"They only did that because they were drunk."
"A real Christian man would never abuse his wife."
"You can't rape someone you're married to."
"If he really assaulted her, she would have told someone right away."

I've heard each of these sentiments personally, all from Christians. And there are many more. These myths permeate our cultural conversations about domestic and interpersonal violence, and the church is particularly saturated with this kind of thinking. And unfortunately, studies have also shown that adherence to these myths does correlate to greater perpetuation of violence.[9]

The study in question examined a group of 238 graduate students from a Protestant evangelical seminary, specifically students with Calvinist beliefs. Reformed theology comprises a very broad and diverse spectrum of beliefs, but here, they're basically talking about the neo-Calvinist resurgence that has happened in the United States among politically and/or socially conservative Christian churches in the last two to three decades. Researchers uncovered two aspects of Calvinist theology that led to increased buy-in to domestic violence myths like those listed above.

The first is a set of *hierarchical relational expectations* that suggests that there is an in-group and an out-group; there is a group that has God's special favor and protection and a group that does not. The in-group is in charge (or they should be), and the out-group must follow. Hierarchical relational expectations are also expressed in interpersonal relationships, especially romantic and sexual ones. There is a leader and a follower. The leader is in charge and the follower is not.

This leads naturally to the second aspect of Calvinist theology that correlates to domestic violence myth acceptance: *complementarian gender ideology*, which I'll discuss in much greater detail in the next chapter. Complementarianism teaches that men and women are technically equal in value in the eyes of God but are required to fulfill very different roles in the home, the church, and broader society. Under complementarianism, it is considered sinful for a woman to do anything, even something seemingly innocuous, that might place her in a position of authority or superiority over a man.

The research showed that commitment to these two ideas led to a greater likelihood of believing myths about domestic and interpersonal violence, noting that "some Christian beliefs overlap with IPVMs"[10] and that "certain Christian beliefs have been implicated as supportive of IPVMs . . . including beliefs historically emphasized within evangelical Protestant theology (e.g., 'female submission and male headship')."[11] Researchers also found that a heightened sense of in-group–out-group identity that comes from placing a high value on hierarchy within relationships reliably predicted adherence to DVMs.[12]

So there's obviously a connection between the theology and the myths. But we're not just talking about semantics here. The research also shows that an acceptance of these violent myths correlates directly to greater rates of domestic violence. And if the myths lead to violence, then the theology leads to violence too. Much of the theology of purity culture is actually just domestic and interpersonal violence myths in Christian disguise.

Many #ChurchToo survivors have expressed some variation of the sentiment that what happened to them was bad, but how their church or religious family members reacted was just as bad if not worse and retraumatized them in extremely powerful ways. The words that were spoken to them in the aftermath of their abuse often constituted a secondary abuse. Language creates reality. And the reality in our churches desperately needs to change.

Imagine if Megan's church leadership had understood that complementarian ideology is actually a risk factor for violent behavior rather than an orthodox belief that must be protected at all costs. Imagine if they had responded in a trauma-informed and survivor-centered way, believing her narrative of her own experience and providing her with the emotional and financial resources to leave the man who had raped her countless times. Imagine if they had looked at her, in the words of Hilary from Into Account, "as someone who has the potential to give the gift of wisdom and justice to the church"?

Sadly, for now, we can only imagine.

—

In the fall of 2018, I got an email I was almost certain was a joke asking me to be interviewed and photographed for an article to be published in the print edition of *Cosmopolitan* magazine. Thanks to the aforementioned Moody Bible Institute internet filters, *Cosmopolitan* magazine was the only way I learned anything about sex during my undergraduate career—and the fact that I was able to learn anything useful from a magazine that publishes sex tips like "put a donut on his penis and eat around it" was nothing short of miraculous. At least I knew what a condom was, which was more than I could say for some of my schoolmates.

But the request was not a joke, and before I knew it, a few days before Christmas, a photographer from Los Angeles was in my backyard taking pictures of me while the journalist was emailing me clarifying questions from our interview about purity culture, healing, and the fallout from Joshua Harris's infamous book *I Kissed Dating Goodbye*. When the magazine hit newsstands in late February, I rushed to my nearest Kroger and bought every copy they had, drove to a bar, bought myself a beer, and nearly pissed myself laughing at the sight of my photo gracing the pages of a magazine whose front cover also advertised "48 sex tweaks you didn't know you needed" and a quiz to find out if you should get bangs.

The article featured three other people, and I knew two of them, my internet friends Dianna and Samantha. But I hadn't met the third, Lyvonne Proverbs Briggs, until our paths crossed in *Cosmopolitan*. I followed her on social media immediately and over the next few months was so inspired by her posts about self-love and healing and the work she was doing with women of color who are survivors of sexual violence. Late that summer as my own divorce was being finalized, I learned from Lyvonne's Instagram posts that she was going through a divorce too, so when I started writing this book, I knew I wanted to schedule a Skype call with her and hear her thoughts about purity culture, sex, the bible, and yes, marriage.

Lyvonne

"So I make it a point to say *penis* in worship as often as possible," Lyvonne stated matter-of-factly, and I burst into laughter. "We have to get comfortable saying these words because language is power." She was telling me a story she'd heard about one of the editors of the New Revised Standard Version (NRSV) of the bible who apparently was aware that the phrase "uncover his feet" in Ruth 3 should most likely be translated as "uncover his penis" but refrained from translating it accurately because the text was to be used in worship and not just academia. But is that not all the more reason to translate it accurately? What you cannot say has power over you.

"I think that in a lot of evangelical spaces, we're using language that is inherently violent and sexist," Lyvonne said, "and that infiltrates our theology and that infiltrates the way that we look at God as well as God's people. It starts with the language and the power that we give to language bearers." I hadn't mentioned the study about Calvinist beliefs and domestic violence to her, but she sure was summarizing it perfectly.

Lyvonne works directly with survivors of sexual violence on a regular basis, so I asked her how she had seen the teachings of purity culture impact the women she works with and the healing process for them. "The silence, stigma, and shame means there's no conversation about what's happening," she said, "and if you're not talking about what's happening, you can't heal from it. . . . The deep healing, the revelation that needs to happen, the confrontation that needs to happen, the acknowledgment, the repentance—just never happens. And you cannot heal if you don't address the wound."

Lyvonne has seen theology hinder the healing process far too often. She said, "For women who've experienced sexual trauma, they then internalize that shame—like it must have been something that they did, or they sinned and God was mad at them, or they shouldn't have been drinking and that's why they got raped, or God is using this to make them stronger—it's a lot of really warped theology!" Instead of offering paths toward healing, our theology is too often contributing to the harm.

"What about marriage?" I asked Lyvonne. "I got divorced because I was gay, not to escape abuse. But even my amicable divorce has given me a lot of feelings about marriage and the way we talk about it. I just feel like about 90 percent of what I was taught about marriage growing up was a lie."

"When I was in the Pentecostal tradition, we spent a lot of time fantasizing about meeting our husbands, getting married, finally being able to have 'legal sex,'" Lyvonne said, "and I witnessed a lot of hyper-Christians getting married at eighteen or nineteen years old just so they could have 'legal sex.' And they were *way* too young, but that's what purity culture does. It says that you can't have sex until you're in a heterosexual marriage—so get in one, and then you're good to go." My experience in bible college was similar. Jokes about getting a "ring by spring" at "Moody Bridal Institute" abounded, and I witnessed several couples get married within a matter of months after they started dating, with varying degrees of long-term success.

But the problem is, "get into a heterosexual marriage and you're good to go," is not true. Lyvonne said, "That doesn't take into account the fact that once you get married, you don't just become this rambunctious sex goddess ready to go at a moment's notice, especially when you've been taught that sex is primarily for men's pleasure. Being taught that you ought to give him sex whenever he wants it leads to marital rape, which some churches won't even acknowledge." I thought again, as I had so many times since we talked, about my interview with Dr. Tina Schermer Sellers, when she had spoken of couples who are "attempting to do a relationship where she's been taught it's all about him, and *he's* been taught it's all about him."

Even outside the context of marriage, the fact that men and women get such different messaging around purity can lead to some incredibly unhealthy, and even dangerous, environments. Both boys and girls are usually instructed to remain abstinent until marriage, but the *language* used varies widely by gender. Girls are usually taught that premarital loss of their "virginity" (almost always meaning penetrative sex involving a penis and a vagina) equates to a loss of value and worth. They become permanently impure, and it's a sin they will never *really* recover from. By contrast, much of the language used to teach boys about purity frames premarital sex in terms of a "mistake"—a lapse in judgment you can recover from and try again. As Lyvonne put it, "If girls are hearing to keep their legs closed and boys are 'allowed' to have sex, then what happens when those two groups get together?" She let the rhetorical question hang in the air for a second and then answered it: "The flames of rape culture are fanned when those two groups get together."

I told Lyvonne about my theory of the modern purity movement emerging as part of the Religious Right's pivot from opposing desegregation to opposing abortion, and I asked her about her thoughts on the connection between purity culture and white supremacy. "Oh, purity culture is *steeped* in white supremacy," she said. "The 'virtuous woman' is probably white and chaste. Black women's bodies have been hypersexualized for millennia."

"A lot of Black churches are 85 percent women," Lyvonne noted. "And when I think about the residual effects of chattel slavery, I think about how our bodies were not our own. Purity culture was not a thing on the continent of Africa. This is something that came with European colonizers and white theologians that was forced upon communities of color. And for women of color, particularly Black women, when the Black church was established as a site of liberation but then becomes a site of oppression, then where are these Black women of faith supposed to get their liberation and healing—if every single system is oppressive for them?"

"Purity culture sucks," she concluded. "Across the board. But you have to have the oppressed espousing the ideology if the system is going to run smoothly. You've gotta get buy-in."

And buy-in requires ignorance. Teach people that you don't question God, then teach people that God is revealed only in the bible, then teach people that the bible can only be interpreted in one particular way—and you've got the perfect recipe for unquestioning obedience. "Getting some Christians to acknowledge that God didn't just gild this bible in the sky and drop it into the hands of Abraham is like—" She halted.

"It's like pulling teeth," I finished.

"Yeah," she said. "It's like pulling teeth."

—

Purity culture's theology of marriage is bleak and dangerous, but it makes perfect sense given what purity culture
teaches about sex and sexuality more generally. Some may
think that if a teaching helps our young people get married
and "cross the finish line" with their sexual purity more or
less intact, then what's the harm? But marriage is not a destination, the path there is not a race, and even if it were,
then you definitely wouldn't want to attempt it without
ever having practiced. Purity culture's theology of marriage
harms people tangibly, measurably, and actively.

As I mentioned in chapter 4, there is basically no teaching
on consent in purity culture because before marriage, you
are always supposed to say no, and after marriage, you don't
have to worry about sinning anymore, so presumably anything goes. Purity culture often treats marriage as a sexual
carte blanche, as is evidenced by the sheer number of books
dedicated to imploring evangelical Christian young people to *not* have sex before marriage but the comparatively
very few books teaching evangelical Christian married couples to have pleasurable sex within marriage. (There are
a few, they are written exclusively for heterosexual couples, and they are not great.) Framing consent as "always
no" in singleness and "always yes" in marriage is a recipe
for abuse and toxic relationship dynamics to take hold.
And while marital rape is technically illegal in all fifty states
(as of 1993), victims of marital rape rarely make a report,
for many of the reasons we have discussed so far. Who
knows how many Christians (statistically speaking, mostly

women) are suffering in silence because they have been told that "the wife does not have authority over her own body, but the husband does" (1 Corinthians 7:4a) means that the husband is entitled to have whatever he wants whenever he wants it.

But it isn't just about sex.

One of the most common refrains you'll hear from people in purity culture talking about marriage is this: "Marriage isn't about happiness; it's about holiness." They say it again and again, almost always when someone is unhappy in their marriage. It's employed as a reminder that since happiness isn't the point, you're not allowed to get divorced just because you're miserable. It's brought up when spousal abuse is revealed, since suffering produces holiness, and holiness is ultimately a good thing. It's given as advice to young couples on their wedding day to let them know that if this union doesn't bring them happiness, they shouldn't get too bent out of shape about it. They'll get their reward in heaven for sticking it out.

But this belief in the irrelevance of happiness in partnered human relationships serves to protect the person in the relationship with the most power and keep both parties docile and playing their parts as cogs in the machine of the purity culture industrial complex. It tells people there's nothing better out there, so why even try? And it plays into that very foundational purity culture belief that pleasure and desire are bad and dangerous, and if you know what's good for you, you'll stay far away from things like following your heart and listening to your body and doing what makes you happy. Happiness is a gateway drug in purity culture. They're afraid that before they know it, you'll think you're worth something. You'll realize you're not fundamentally broken and you don't need a cure for a disease you don't have. And if you can figure that out on your own, then what do you need them for?

"What are y'all out here doing?" Lyvonne asked toward the end of our conversation. "Being married and just trying to get to a year where you don't despise each other? 'Cause I'm not interested." I couldn't have said it better than that.

Your happiness matters. Whether you are a survivor of sexualized violence or not, whether you are married or not, your happiness matters, and it is worth fighting for. Yes, #ChurchToo is about breaking down the oppressive ways that people construct marriages and fighting for survivors of spousal abuse who have been told by their churches that their stories do not matter. But #ChurchToo is also about pleasure. Pleasure, fully experienced and freely savored, is quite the antidote to shame.

8

I SUFFER NOT A WOMAN

But I suffer not a woman to teach, nor to usurp authority over the man, but to be in silence. For Adam was first formed, then Eve.

—1 Timothy 2:12 KJV

Obey your leaders and submit to them, for they are keeping watch over your souls and will give an account.

—Hebrews 13:17a

Those committed to the theology of complementarianism can do very little, if anything, to solve the problem of #ChurchToo.

That's not true, of course, if you ask them. Complementarians everywhere have gone to great lengths to talk about how much they care about survivors of sexual violence and just how dedicated they are to doing the right thing when a survivor comes forward in their church. "Our churches must have clearer policies about sexual abuse," they cry! "Pastors must make a formal report when the law requires it! Pastors should be trained in how to care for survivors when they come forward!" And all of that is, technically, very true. But the basic tenets of complementarianism are fundamentally at odds with building a world in which women, LGBTQ and nonbinary persons, and survivors of all genders are seen as equal.

Thanks to my degree from Moody Bible Institute, I'm very familiar with how to define and describe complementarianism charitably. Complementarianism is the theology that says that while God created both men and women as equally valuable, worthy, and loved, men and women have different roles to fill in the home, church, and broader society that are not interchangeable with one another. Men are to lead; women are to follow. Men are to initiate; women are to accept. Men are to be strong, decisive, and straightforward; women are to be soft, compliant, and strategic.

The Danvers Statement, first published by the Council on Biblical Manhood and Womanhood (CBMW) in 1988 and considered by many to be the premier document outlining the evangelical theology of gender complementarity, puts it this way: "Both Adam and Eve were created in God's image, equal before God as persons and distinct in their manhood and womanhood. . . . Distinctions in masculine and feminine roles are ordained by God as part of the created order, and should find an echo in every human heart."[1] *Should* being the operative word in that sentence.

This affirmation of equality in value and difference in roles is meant to reflect the way that Jesus lovingly leads, corrects, and guides his church[2]—a metaphor in which men play the part of Jesus and women play the part of the church. Obviously, this strict gender divide implies that there only *are* two genders: cisgender men and cisgender women. Persons who desire romantic and sexual relationships with people of the same gender as well as persons whose gender identity falls outside of that binary have no home in complementarianism. Even straight and cisgender men and women whose natural talents or aspirations do not align with those assigned to them based on their genitals—such as men who are stay-at-home fathers or women who have gifts of leadership and delegation—run the risk of being censured.

Complementarianism is a grossly unequal system masquerading as an equal one. It *says* that men and women are equal, but they don't appear to be equal at all based on how they are treated. No outsider would ever look at a church where only men can serve as spiritual leaders and where women are to submit to their husbands in all marital decisions and think, *Wow, this is truly a community where men and women are equal in value!* The actual *outcome* of complementarian ideology is not gender parity, and it is certainly not justice for women, sexual minorities, and other marginalized groups harmed by these patriarchal expectations. And in the words of Jesus, "Thus you will know them by their fruits" (Matthew 7:20).

And yet, even though the pillars of complementarian theology are at odds with what is required to heal the wounds of sexualized violence in our churches, many complementarians who self-identify as staunch supporters of survivors of sexual violence feel no cognitive dissonance between these oppositional commitments. To be fair, many of them aren't really referring to #ChurchToo survivors when they talk about survivors of sexualized violence. A lot of times, when complementarians talk about sexual violence, what they mean is sex trafficking (and usually also sex work, which is not the same thing but is often treated as such in contexts where consent is seen as an irrelevant factor in the morality of any given sexual act). I don't have the time or space in this book to offer a complete analysis of the primarily white, evangelical obsession with "saving" victims of global and domestic sex trafficking, but the obsession itself must be noted here due to the way that opposition to sex trafficking often functions to absolve evangelical Christians of any responsibility for the sexual violence that takes place in their communities. Many complementarians are far more comfortable talking about sexual violence that is happening "out there" than about the sexual violence that is happening in their midst.

And when complementarians *do* admit that perhaps there are survivors of sexual violence sitting in their pews, the violence is usually framed as having been inflicted by an outsider. As the #MeToo hashtag first went viral in the fall of 2017, my newsfeed was full of complementarians gleefully decrying the wickedness of "the world" and the fall of various Hollywood celebrities and politicians, reminding everyone that sexual deviancy is a natural result of failing to follow God's perfect plan for sex and gender as clearly outlined in their interpretation of the bible. The implication was that those who follow this mythical plan would never abuse or be abused—a "No True Christian" fallacy, if you will. Sadly, acknowledgment that predators sit in their pews and stand in their pulpits unchecked is often far from their lips.

Complementarianism builds a culture of sexualized violence through its twin emphases on male headship and female submission. Its adherents often claim that it's only a *misinterpretation* of male headship and female submission that leads to abuse, but the data we have doesn't bear that out (see the discussion about the correlation between conservative beliefs about gender and acceptance of domestic violence myths in chapter 7). This is especially evident when you look at complementarian teachings about sex within marriage, which sometimes go so far as to question whether it is ever appropriate for a woman to tell her husband no in bed. "Sex is integral to the marriage relationship," as one conservative commentator put it. "It is due . . . a right, happily owed by one another to one another."[3]

A system that conditions women to devalue their own *no* in favor of what a man wants (or what they are told God "wants" as relayed through a man) is a system that is ripe for abuse. And ultimately, those rigid gender roles are bad for everyone of every gender—men included. But because complementarianism is seen as synonymous with biblical truth in many circles—and because the bible is seen as inerrant—getting people to have that conversation is difficult to say the least. Complementarian pastor and teacher Ed Stetzer, in an article for *Christianity Today* promoting a "summit" he organized about #ChurchToo issues, said, "Some will say that evangelical beliefs are the problem, and we particularly understand that may come from some who have been hurt by evangelical churches."[4]

In other words, if you think the theology is the problem, it's probably just because you were hurt. There would never be a solid intellectual or spiritual reason to disagree, of course. This maneuver, too, is a function of the covert misogyny that is inherent in the complementarian theological system. Because women are seen as more "emotional" than men, being emotional is bad because it's coded as female—and opposing certain theologies for supposedly emotional reasons, such as being hurt, is invalid because it doesn't meet the rigorous and unemotional male standard of "objectivity." But while there are plenty of good intellectual and spiritual reasons to reject complementarianism, there are good emotional ones too.

The way that complementarianism dichotomizes those with power and those without it can wreak havoc on survivors of sexualized violence in the church. When the men in charge are seen as holy men of God with special access to the divine will—and when those same men are taught from birth that they are entitled to call the shots sexually—destruction naturally ensues. It is, as they say, a feature, not a bug.

—

"He's a narcissist," Jules said, gesturing with both hands. "And he cannot keep his mouth shut. So I knew he was gonna dig himself a hole. And that's exactly what he did."

"Oh my god," I butted in. "When that *Mother Jones* article[5] came out, I could not believe he actually gave them a quote! I couldn't believe he said something!"

"That quote!" Jules shouted. She suddenly took on a lower voice, impersonating her abuser, Andy, as she rolled her eyes back in her head. "'I supported the #MeToo movement, but the #ChurchToo movement seems a little too aggressive and attacking,'[6] like—fuck you, dude!" We both burst into laughter.

I couldn't help but smile. The Jules I was seeing on my laptop screen was different—in a good way—than the Jules the media had often portrayed.

For the first couple of months when #ChurchToo began going viral, most of the stories being shared were from people just like me: individuals who had experienced abuse at churches most people had never heard of at the hands of perpetrators most people had never heard of. But when Jules came forward in January 2018 with her story of being sexually assaulted by her youth pastor while she was in high school, #ChurchToo was launched into the spotlight in a new way. Her abuser, Andy Savage, was a popular mega-church pastor in the Memphis area and had a big conference coming up as well as a forthcoming book about marriage. He was a rising evangelical celebrity and a household name in his area. I watched the hashtag obsessively that week, eager to see what this community we had spent the last couple of months building could do.

Thanks to the relentless activism of countless individuals working under the #ChurchToo banner, it wasn't long before Andy's church was forced to address the allegations against him. The church live-streamed their service that Sunday, as they always did, and thousands of viewers across the country watched in horror as Andy stood on stage, admitted to a "sexual incident" with Jules, and then received a standing ovation from the congregation for his honesty and penitence.

Watching an entire congregation applaud a pastor for admitting to sexual assault of a minor in his spiritual care ignited the rage of #ChurchToo supporters all around the world, and headlines about Jules's story dominated news-feeds for weeks. Jules made her media debut in a video for the *New York Times* in March, where they played the recording of Andy's nonapology and subsequent ovation, capturing Jules's responses and thoughts in real time. Most of the time in the video, she was looking down. I remember thinking she had a distinctly demure air. She was muted even in the way that she wept gracefully, in the way that she squeezed her French-tipped hands together whenever Andy started to speak on the recording.

But the Jules I saw in front of me now was different. She was messy and raw and her eyes lit up when she talked. It was the day after Christmas, and she was Skyping me from the house she and her family had rented in New Mexico for the holidays.

"So what was your church like growing up—the church where Andy was your pastor?" I asked her. "What did they teach about women and sex?"

"In that church," Jules said, "I grew up learning that women are to be submissive, that the man is the head of the household—you know that umbrella drawing, where it's like God, and then the man, and then the wife and then the kids?"

"The Bill Gothard illustration,[7] yeah," I said.

"It was like that. And then as I came of age as a teenager, we had a youth group, and purity culture was huge. We did True Love Waits every year as a weekend event—Andy taught that—and we had the purity rings. And one of the big teachings of True Love Waits is that it's not just sexual purity that's important but your thoughts as well. So you shouldn't even *think* about these things, and if you did think about them, it was wrong and sinful. So that was very much the culture I grew up in. It was very much about male headship and all that traditional conservative theology."

"Even in my own parents' relationship, my mom was quite submissive to my dad. Then my parents ended up getting divorced my junior year right before my assault—" She paused and took a sip of her water. "Oh, I was also raped my junior year of high school before Andy assaulted me, and I had confided in Andy about all of that."

I stopped to pick my jaw up off the floor. "Sorry, what?" That fact had not made it into any of the articles that had been written about Jules and her story. "So you were assaulted by someone else, and he knew about that?"

"Yeah," she said. "When I came forward initially, I didn't want people to focus on the fact that I had been raped before. It was my junior year at prom, and I had felt responsible. So I didn't share that, but . . ." Jules's train of thought petered off. "It does make it so much worse to know that he did know that about me, but it doesn't change the fact that what he did was wrong."

I nodded, a fuller picture forming in my mind of just how ugly what Andy had done to Jules—and what her church had worked to cover up—had been.

"So when Andy assaulted me," Jules said, "I reported it to the associate pastor within twenty-four hours. And as I sat in the associate pastor's office bawling my eyes out, the first thing he said to me was, 'So you're telling me you participated.' And I knew in that moment I was being blamed. They were going to treat it as a mutual thing. The associate pastor promised me that the church would handle it with Andy, but they didn't do anything." Jules told me that Andy taught the True Love Waits program again right after she reported him to the associate pastor and that the only reason he was eventually "allowed to resign" was because the parents of a girl in her girls' small group found out about the report Jules had made. Even then, the church still threw him a going-away party—and she was still seen as the horrible person that let the big secret out.

"But these were the most godly men. They were to be respected. They were the leaders," she said. "That was a thing I felt like a lot of people really misunderstood. When I told my story, I said the reason I did what I did when Andy asked me to was because I thought that meant he loved me. And a lot of people took that to mean that it was consensual. But the culture that I grew up in taught that the only reason that a sexual act should occur was within true love.

So that's how I was manipulated. In my seventeen-year-old mind, the only way I could justify what he was asking me to do was to think that he must love me. But compliance is not consent."

"You almost have to deal with the cognitive dissonance by creating a fantasy," I remarked offhandedly, thinking of my own sixteen-year-old beliefs about my abuser's wisdom and character and about the "fawn" response to trauma. "Because if there's no fantasy, then this person that you respect is a bad person doing a bad thing."

"Exactly," Jules said. "And who doesn't want true love with the most godly man in your life?"

—

The church where Jules's youth pastor was allowed to prey on her was a Southern Baptist Church, a denomination that has seen hundreds of accusations of clergy sexual abuse, assault, and harassment come to light in recent years[8] and that is stridently complementarian in every aspect of church life. The Southern Baptist Convention has gone so far as to formally kick out churches that have dared to hire female pastors (although somehow it cannot seem to wield the same unflinching ecclesiastical authority over member churches that harbor sexual predators).[9]

But I do not want anyone to walk away from this book with the idea that it is *only* complementarians, with their retrogressive gender roles and Amelia Bedelia hermeneutics of the Pauline epistles, who have a problem with sexualized violence in their communities. Complementarianism may be a specific set of very dangerous and troubling theological beliefs. But complementarianism is also a mindset. You don't have to believe that women can't be pastors to have a community characterized by patriarchy, misogyny, and violence that is not safe for survivors.

Complementarianism is merely one specific evangelical Christian codification of misogyny. But there are plenty of progressive Christians, especially progressive men, who sit around poking fun at how backward complementarianism is while failing to hold the predatory men around them accountable for their violent actions and viewing women with a disdain and disbelief that would rival any Southern Baptist Church in the country. You can adopt the spirit of complementarianism even if you have a woman in the pulpit and a rainbow flag on your church website.

Bill Hybels, former pastor of Willow Creek Community Church in Chicago, one of the first evangelical megachurches to ordain women, was forced to resign after allegations of sexual misconduct came to light in 2018. Hybels had been a spiritual advisor to President Bill Clinton and a vocal supporter of women in ministry.

And in 2019 Christian speaker and "comedian" John Crist, whose videos often focused on poking fun at the oddities of evangelical Christianity, was finally toppled after *years* of young women trying to come forward about the ways that he had used his celebrity status to abuse, manipulate, assault, and prey upon them.

And most recently, in the summer of 2020, progressive Christian Enneagram guru Chris Heuertz, who spent much of his early ministry advocating for victims of global sex trafficking, was publicly accused of abuse and misconduct of various kinds, including sexual, by thirty-three individuals.[10] Powerful figures such as Brené Brown, Richard Rohr, and others began to distance themselves from him in the wake of the accusations, and his publisher suspended promotions for his upcoming book. But as more information about Heuertz's behavior came out in the days and weeks that followed, it became abundantly clear that like Harvey Weinstein's assistants who escorted women to his hotel rooms, there was a whole host of people who knew about Heuertz's predations and chose to do nothing—or even intentionally promoted him and worked to expand his influence.

Progressive men in particular can benefit from looking like the "good guys," all while behaving in ways that are anything but progressive behind closed doors. Many will say that they believe women are equal, but the way they interact with the actual women in their lives often looks more like it is informed by complementarianism than a commitment to gender and sexual justice.

It's easy for progressive Christians to point a finger at fundamentalist or conservative evangelical churches and denominations that have been implicated in sexual abuse cases, feeling good about themselves because their theology of sexuality and gender is so much more evolved and in line with modern science and medicine. But progressive theology is not a vaccination against sexual violence—and it can often serve as the perfect cover for predators. Progressive churches should ask themselves where and how the complementarian ideals of misogyny, violence, and patriarchal power-hoarding show up in their day-to-day community life. Making churches safe for marginalized people like women, children, and LGBTQ folks is predicated on examining the power structures that are modeled as normative and healthy. A complementarian church will certainly never be "safe." But a church is also not safe simply because it is progressive. Rejecting complementarianism is only the first step.

—

Toward the end of our conversation on Skype, I asked Jules about what happened *after* the assault and the subsequent mishandling of it by her church—how she coped and survived for all those years before coming forward publicly in January 2018.

"I totally compartmentalized it and tried to move on, but the depression and anxiety became so great that I ended up having to leave college, where I was getting my pilot's license, because I was just such a hot mess," Jules said. Most people familiar with Jules's story know she is a flight attendant. But she started college wanting to be a pilot.

"I didn't understand what depression or anxiety was," she continued. "I didn't understand that's what I was experiencing. I would just lock myself in my room, and I started cutting. So I went back to Texas and transferred schools, and it was there that I finally sought help through the school counselor. I was cutting so bad that they involuntarily committed me to the psych ward, and I was there for a week. But it saved my life because I finally got the help that I needed and got on meds and into therapy."

I told Jules about how after my abuse disclosure was botched by my parents and my church, I left town for three months. By the time I came back, I had dissociated from what had happened to me so thoroughly that I just didn't talk about it and pretended like I was "healed." The alternative would have been to admit that my church leaders and my parents had failed morally, and I couldn't do that. "But it was like—" I paused, thinking. "It was like I broke my leg, and the bone never quite set right. But I learned how to walk again. Even if it was with a limp."

"Yeah," Jules said. "It was like a broken bone that never set right for me too. I was dealing with my depression and anxiety, but I hadn't dealt with the underlying causes and the trauma I'd suffered. I felt like I could talk about it, but I didn't have a good handle on it. He was still in charge. He got to control the narrative. I wasn't in control of that part of my story. And that's what I finally was able to take back when I went public."

"And it was really the secular world that brought attention to my story," Jules noted.

"No, it wasn't Christian media, that's for sure!" I said. "Christians had zero interest in touching #ChurchToo stories for the longest time."

"Exactly. It was the secular world that ended up having my back," Jules said, "and pushing the story out there and saying 'this is wrong.' The church has refused to talk about these issues. And not only have they refused to call out perpetrators, but they refuse to talk about the culture and the theology behind abuse and the toxic environment that has created this monster."

I watched on Skype as Jules picked up her phone, rummaged through her purse, walked out to the balcony of their rental house, and lit a cigarette. "Why do you think that is?" I asked her. "Why do you think Christians are so hesitant to engage in conversations about changing their theology?"

"Because they have to admit they're wrong," Jules said. "They have to admit they're evolving. But I'm evolving in this, Emily. I'm evolving in my healing journey; I'm evolving in my story being public. I don't have a handbook on how to do this. And there wasn't a handbook for me. You just kind of learn as you go. And I'm feeling more confident in telling even more personal details of my story now than I did before, and that's part of my healing journey too. I'm constantly evolving in this."

I smiled. "I can see that," I said. "It's a good look."

—

I'll say one thing for complementarianism: it's got a killer marketing team. I'm hard-pressed to think of another doctrine that didn't exist a few decades ago that now enjoys such a cozy, right-hand seat next to orthodoxy.

But as with the other doctrines I've covered so far, divesting from this one is *crucial* to solving the problem of #ChurchToo. The fantasy of being able to hold onto all the theologies that create cultures of sexualized violence and still work to end that sexualized violence is tantalizing, but it's deadly. You wouldn't expect to be able to run a marathon if you never got off the couch and started training. You have to do the work, even if the work, like running, is not fun, sexy, glamorous, or easy.

But it is easy for those who have never experienced sexualized violence in the church to merely opt out of this work because it is difficult and uncomfortable. Complementarianism, like homophobia, often acts as a theological purity test that evangelical Christians use to determine whether others are Christian enough. So much is at stake socially when it comes to questioning this seemingly sacrosanct doctrine.

What I would like for complementarians and those afraid to question them to remember is that there was a lot at stake for me when I was groomed by my abuser and blamed for it by my parents. And there was a lot at stake for Jules when Andy assaulted her on that back road and her church said she participated. And there was a lot at stake for every single survivor of sexualized violence who was told that it was somehow their fault because they didn't play the God-ordained role assigned to them based on their genitals well enough.

There has *been* a lot at stake. Not all of us have had the luxury—or the privilege—of choosing not to risk it.

Standing in solidarity with the marginalized looks like making yourself uncomfortable in order to do the right thing. It looks like risking your faith as you know it to honor your own humanity and the humanity in others, trusting that there is faith on the other side too. It looks like finally, finally learning how to love people more than you love your ideas about God and finding out that that is actually how you love God anyway. If I may be so bold, it looks like losing your life to find it.

Nothing is as simple as complementarianism makes it out to be. We are people, not genitalia-specific robots. Our talents, our desires, our hopes and dreams, and what we need to be happy are as unique as our fingerprints. We can do so much better than this. And for the sake of survivors of sexualized violence who bear the scars of institutionalized misogyny, violence, and power-hoarding—we must.

—

One of the last things Jules and I talked about in our interview was justice. The statute of limitations for the crime committed against Jules had long since passed. Like me, she had very little legal recourse when she came forward.

"What's justice for you?" I asked.

"Justice is ugly. Justice is not clean. Justice is not cookie-cutter," Jules said. "I knew that I would never see justice in the form of a legal case."

"Thankfully that's not the only kind of justice," I responded. "Because guess what happens when you type the name 'Andy Savage' into Google?"

"And that's my justice," Jules said victoriously. "I took my story back."

9

GREATER LOVE

Greater love has no one than this: to lay down one's life for one's friends.

—John 15:13 NIV

If another member of the church sins against you, go and point out the fault when the two of you are alone. If the member listens to you, you have regained that one. But if you are not listened to, take one or two others along with you, so that every word may be confirmed by the evidence of two or three witnesses.

—Matthew 18:15–16

Certain species of pelicans have a little red tip on the ends of their beaks. A Christian legend dating back to medieval times says their beaks are red because when a mother pelican cannot find enough food for her young, she will pierce her own breast and feed them with her own flesh. Pelicans don't actually do this, but understandably, this myth caused the pelican to become a popular early Christian symbol of Jesus and his sacrifice. Dante and Aquinas both referred to Jesus as a pelican in their writings, and there are paintings of Queen Elizabeth I of England wearing the symbol of the pelican on her dress.

And, I mean, the idea is sort of romantic, in a dysfunctional, self-immolating kind of way. Back when I thrived on chaos and self-loathing and thought that setting myself on fire to keep my idea of God warm was the point of the Christian life, I would have eaten that shit right up. Radical selflessness in the supposed service of others, even to the point of death? Swoon. But dysfunction aside, there's a bigger problem here. The metaphor of the pelican doesn't only get applied to Jesus Christ. The pelican as a metaphor is fundamentally coded as feminine, as it's always a *mother* bird tearing into herself to feed her young.

Messaging about self-sacrifice and self-effacement geared toward women in the evangelical church is widespread. Working in a church office, I have the distinct privilege of being the one to open all the mail, and whenever Christian book catalogs come in, I usually take a few minutes to peruse the pages out of morbid curiosity. The gendered messaging for women is as stark as it is bleak. Titles encouraging women to pray harder, be more selfless, and make the best of their current situation without doing anything to change it abound. "Choose joy!" they say. Fret less. Read your bible more. But never, under any circumstances, try to take your happiness into your own hands and get out of a situation that is making you miserable. That's for selfish people. That's for men.

But recently, one group of evangelical women went even further and formed something called the Pelican Project.

The Pelican Project is a self-described "guild" of evangelical women, primarily writers and theologians, that exists to offer resources to other evangelical women and foster commitment to local evangelical churches.

Several of the founding members were interviewed on *Christianity Today*'s website when the Pelican Project was first announced in November 2018. The interviewer asked Kristie Anyabwile (wife of Thabiti Anyabwile, the pastor and Gospel Coalition contributor who famously said that Christians ought to have a "gag reflex" when they think about LGBTQ relationships[1]) about the significance of the pelican metaphor. "The image is both Christological and feminine," she said.[2] In Christianity, tearing the flesh out of your own breast to feed other people is a way to be like Jesus—but it's also specifically a way to be like Jesus as a woman. And while there are many metaphors for Jesus, the feminine-coded ones are more likely to include elements of self-sacrifice than are the masculine-coded ones.[3]

In their incredible book *Burnout: The Secret to Unlocking the Stress Cycle*,[4] health educator Dr. Emily Nagoski and her sister, professor and conductor Amelia Nagoski, talk about patriarchy as a stressor using the language of "Human Giver Syndrome," an idea they borrowed from feminist philosopher Kate Manne in her book *Down Girl: The Logic of Misogyny*.[5] Manne talks about two classes of people: the human givers and the human beings. Unpacking this idea in their own book, the Nagoskis write, "The human givers are expected to offer their time, attention, affection and bodies willingly, placidly, to the other class of people: the human beings. The implication in these terms is that human beings have a moral obligation to be or express their humanity, while human givers have a moral obligation to give their humanity to the human beings. Guess which one women are?"[6]

I agree with the Nagoskis that this human giver / human being dichotomy is something that affects women significantly and negatively, especially in Christian churches. But I also observe that Human Giver Syndrome, as a function of patriarchy, applies to all relationships where there is a dominant/subordinate hierarchy or where one party is perceived as "strong" and the other party is perceived as "weak." "Givers," the Nagoskis go on to say, "are expected to abdicate any resource or power they may happen to acquire, their jobs, their love, their bodies—those belong to the beings. Human givers must at all times be pretty, happy, calm, generous, and attentive to the needs of others—which means they must never be ugly, angry, upset, ambitious, or attentive to their own needs."[7]

This Human Giver Syndrome is at the heart of the interactions that so many survivors of all genders have with their abusers, their churches, their parents, and others in power over them. Miguel De La Torre, speaking about the way men of color have historically been objectified and feminized as a way of furthering global colonial conquest, wrote, "All these forms of oppression [racism, sexism, classism] are identical in their attempt to domesticate others; that is, to place the Other in the subordinate position," and one method of that subordination is to assign the Other "passive characteristics so they could occupy the feminine space."[8] What De La Torre applies to colonialism can also be applied to sexualized violence. The survivor—whether female, male, nonbinary, or any other gender identity—is placed in the position of the Other, the subordinate, the feminine, the weak, the human giver. And the survivor is expected to sacrifice themselves on the behalf of their abuser, the human being. "And if a giver doesn't obediently and sweetly hand over what a being wants," the Nagoskis write, "for that, too, the giver may be punished, shamed, or even destroyed."[9]

It is from this poisonous milieu that the Christian theology of interpersonal sin and forgiveness emerges. Largely taken from Jesus's instructions as recorded in the Gospel of Matthew, many if not most Christian churches teach that when someone has sinned against you, your first line of defense is to confront them about their offense privately, directly, and individually. If they refuse to acknowledge what they've done, Jesus says, the next step is to take along a friend or two "so that every word may be confirmed by the evidence of two or three witnesses" (Matthew 18:16b). As a last resort, Jesus says that the offending party's sin can be told to the entire assembly, and if that doesn't work, then "let such a one be to you as a Gentile and a tax collector" (Matthew 18:17b). Oooh, burn.

From a clinical and practical standpoint, *this is a terrible (and illegal!) way to deal with sexual crimes.* Survivors of sexual assault should not have to privately confront those who abused them, and very few sexual crimes will ever be confirmed by multiple witnesses, since they are often committed in isolation. Additionally, many states have mandatory reporting laws that apply to clergy, so going through the whole process that Jesus lays out in Matthew 18 without making a report immediately would constitute an additional crime. However, many churches take these teachings of Jesus literally and apply them to instances of sexualized violence in their midst because they do not acknowledge the difference between a *crime* and a *sin.*

To many conservative Christians, all wrongdoing is sin, and all sin is the same in the eyes of God. From an early age, I was taught at home and in Sunday school that if I was the only person who ever existed, Jesus would still have had to die on the cross for my sins. The implication is that the "sins" you committed in early childhood—fighting with your siblings, failing to obey your parents the first time they told you to do something, and so on—were enough to justify the violence of the crucifixion. Ironically, because all sin in this framework (no matter how big or small) is enough to justify the violence of the crucifixion, the very idea of "sin" gets flattened out and the word itself ceases to have much meaning at all. If stealing a cookie from the cookie jar and committing mass murder have the same divine moral weight and the same result—Jesus on the cross—then we can mean nothing practically using a word like *sin* to describe both actions. *Sin* no longer refers to something that might have a measurable effect outside of itself—it merely becomes a catchall term that refers to anything that the speaker's particular interpretation of the bible defines as wrongdoing.

So when, for example, a pastor sexually assaults a congregant, usually his action is seen as a sin (if it is acknowledged at all). But if, say, the woman he assaulted was in the habit of coming to church wearing low-cut tops, that immodesty would likely also be defined as a sin. She was also having marital problems, so she probably wasn't being very submissive to her husband, which is yet another sin. On top of that, she is very angry now and saying negative things about the pastor and the church on social media, so she's not following the process of confrontation Jesus laid out in Matthew 18—even more sins. Ultimately, their sins cancel each other out. "Both sides" sinned, and since he's apologizing, she needs to repent of her anger and forgive him so that they can both just move on from this unfortunate incident. Besides, the pastor has been used mightily by God to advance the gospel, and if this bitter woman keeps making a big deal out of this, she's going to harm his future ministry. Her feelings are not more important than the work he has to do for the kingdom of God, after all!

Sound familiar? That's because this is how it's played out time after time. The details change, but the principles stay the same. Survivors—human givers—are expected to forgive and sacrifice themselves on the altar of some larger cause, because their abusers—the human beings—have a moral obligation to continue their work in the world. And this specter of self-sacrifice looms large on the horizon of so many survivors' minds. Many of us have been trained from birth that putting yourself last is the only way to be a moral person in the eyes of God. We have been taught that emulating Jesus means allowing ourselves to be crucified. We have been discipled in a tradition that romanticizes a bird that tears meat out of its own breast to feed others.

But this emphasis on self-sacrifice to the point of self-annihilation never seems to apply to perpetrators of sexual violence. In the Christian context, perpetrators almost always occupy a space of privilege, so they are the ones that get the exceptions. We let their sins slide while survivors are held to the harshest and most woodenly translated version of the biblical text. I don't like it when Jesus is used like a dead relative to justify whatever the speaker was going to do anyway ("Oh, it's what he would have wanted"). And I don't know if it's possible to know exactly what Jesus or the author of Matthew meant in chapter 18. But it seems clear to me that the Jesus who preached things like "blessed are the poor in spirit" and "blessed are those who mourn" and "blessed are the pure in heart" just a few chapters earlier would not advocate for a system in which survivors of sexual violence are kept in bondage and silence and their abusers go free.

Forgiveness is a gift you give to yourself, when and if you are ready. It is not obligatory, and it should not hold you hostage. It is certainly not something you must sacrifice your own health or well-being to extend to someone else. The idea of "human givers" and "human beings" is a useful sociological description of the phenomena at play in Christian churches today. But in reality, everyone is a human being. No one is required to sacrifice themselves in order to make sure someone else's life and work go on uninterrupted. And the idea that *anyone* might be expected to is, in itself, a function of patriarchy and a symptom of purity culture.

—

At first glance, the theology around forgiveness and self-sacrifice that is so popular in many churches might seem unrelated to purity culture. But it's deeply connected, and not just because the expectation to forgive is disproportionately applied to women and other marginalized groups. One of the main precepts of purity culture is that your individual feelings—what you need, what you want, what's good for you, what's healthy for your mind and body—do not matter. All that matters is what the bible says or is purported to say.

So in order to be a good Christian, you must lay all your desires and concerns for your own health and well-being on the altar, light a match, and walk away. I think of how, when I was younger, I was terrified that God was going to call me to marry someone I wasn't attracted to, and I would just have to do it because it was God's will. I went on several extremely unnecessary dates in college for that very reason.

Ultimately, the idea that your desires and your health must be subsumed under a bigger cause like "God's will" or "what the bible says" serves to maintain the existing power structures of purity culture and conservative evangelical Christianity more generally and to keep adherents obedient and placid. Because these expectations are never applied to those with power and privilege (at least not to the extent they are applied to marginalized groups), they serve as a protector of that very power and privilege. Remember De La Torre's concept of a "feminine space." The majority of survivors of sexual violence are, of course, women—82 percent of juvenile survivors and 90 percent of adult survivors.[10] But men and survivors of other genders are not immune from being placed in the feminine space and asked to give up everything, even their very lives. Whoever is placed in that "lesser" space will always have their lives demanded of them for the sake of those in power, whether that is a teenage lesbian who is told that she must never have a romantic relationship because her church believes the bible requires it or a congregant who is told they must forgive their abusive pastor so they don't ruin his reputation. And spoiler alert: survivors of sexualized violence are always, always placed in that "lesser" space, regardless of gender.

Lyvonne, whom I interviewed in chapter 7, said something near the end of our conversation that stuck with me. "Who does that serve?" she asked. "To have these twenty-first-century handmaidens running around? It doesn't serve women, that's for sure." The only benefit of purity culture for women is for white women. By adhering to the teachings of purity culture, they can get closer to heterosexual white male power and privilege and in some ways approximate that power and privilege for themselves, in their own limited spheres. But they do this at the expense of their health and their souls—and at the expense of other women. In the end, purity culture doesn't really serve them either. And it certainly doesn't serve women of color, men of color, LGBTQ Christians, or other marginalized groups within Christianity—especially survivors of sexualized violence.

The requirements of purity culture are unhealthy and, in some cases, even dangerous for the human body and the human mind. But in the context of purity culture, that doesn't matter. "What is healthy" is far less important than "what is biblical." So when an act of sexual violence is committed within the context of purity culture, it is no surprise when the survivor is asked to forget about what is healthy for them and instead do what is required. This phenomenon is simply an extension of the misogynist logic of purity culture, wherein survivors take on the feminine Other and are asked to lay down their lives.

—

I think sometimes people who haven't experienced the dark underbelly of the church for themselves don't get how bad it can be. There are many thousands of tweets under the #ChurchToo tag, and not all of them deal with the topic of forgiveness, but many do. These are just a few of the real-life stories shared under the #ChurchToo banner. There are countless more. They should horrify, convict, and move us to action. All tweets are shared with permission.

I was raped when I was 9 by a member of my church. The pastor, and my parents, told me I needed to forgive him, as that is what Jesus would do. They made me hug my rapist and tell him I forgave him. #churchtoo

—@darcorina[11]

My youth pastor was convicted of "child enticement w/ intent to have sexual contact" w/ a 12-year-old girl. A scared mother went to a church meeting for info. Instead, she said she watched him be hugged and told by every church leader: "We forgive you, we forgive you . . ." #churchtoo

—@LindaKayKlein[12]

When your pastor's son rapes you and you are told by your female youth leader you should have just sat down with him and had a conversation with him . . . hear his side & forgive him, like Jesus would do, instead of speaking out and pressing charges. #churchtoo #wwjd

—Anonymous Twitter User[13]

Because I was told if I didn't forgive my perpetrator, my sins wouldn't be forgiven and I would not get to go to Heaven. #WhyIDidntReport #ChurchToo #MeToo

—@DaisyRainMartin[14]

#Churchtoo exists because if you put Christian survivors of partner abuse in a room together and ask "who here was told by their pastors to forgive their rapist or God won't forgive you your sins?" all the hands go up. I'm not exaggerating. I sat in this room and raised my hand.

—@ThatMandyNicole[15]

I was in an abusive relationship in high school, but I was told to acknowledge my role in the sexual abuse and that I should forgive him, and marry him, because I would never find another Christian man that loved me after what I had done. #ChurchToo

—@mandster60[16]

My friend was raped by her youth pastor. She told the church leadership. Turned out she was the 3rd victim. Their solution? She should forgive him; and she and the other victims should stand before the congregation with their attacker and say it was consensual. #churchtoo

—@bougiefeminist[17]

#churchtoo

I was at summer camp a week after being drugged and rape (at 17). I confessed it to my camp counselor and she told me God doesn't count rape as losing my virginity as long as I forgive the person who raped me. #sofuckedup

—@lilmermaidtiff[18]

—

When Southern Baptist celebrity and theological giant Paige Patterson was finally ousted from power, it was due in large part to a survivor of campus sexual assault who came forward to the news media in 2018. The woman had been assaulted at Southeastern Baptist Theological Seminary in 2003, when Patterson was president. She shared the story of how the man she was dating at the time, another student, assaulted her after being invited into her apartment. When she reported the assault to the school, Patterson counseled her to forgive her assailant. No report was ever filed, and the woman was placed on probation for two years, presumably for violating the seminary's policy that prohibited being alone with a man in her apartment.[19]

I say "finally" ousted from power because reports about Patterson's misogyny and maltreatment of women had been circulating for years. There's an easily accessible video of him preaching at a Southern Baptist conference in Las

Vegas in 2014, where he overtly sexualizes a sixteen-year-old girl he's telling a story about, to raucous laughter from the audience.[20] He was also well known, à la John Piper, for counseling abused women to stay with their abusive husbands and submit to them in all things. In 2000, he told the story at a conference of a woman who came to church with two black eyes after he'd counseled her to stay with her husband. "I hope you're happy!" she reportedly said to him. Patterson responded that he was happy, because her husband had heard her prayers and finally come to church with her for the first time.[21] In true giver/being fashion, the abusive husband's spiritual health was more important than the abused wife's safety, which she must give up to nourish him.

So it's no surprise that Patterson would tell a survivor of sexual assault that she must forgive the man who assaulted her and punish her for the part she supposedly played. In some ways, it feels like Patterson and all the church leaders and school officials and Christian parents who have ever coerced the words "I forgive you" from the lips of survivors are reading out of the same playbook—because they are. The threads of purity culture and patriarchy run strong and true through the fabric of Christian culture. They connect the seemingly unconnected, so two people in two different churches who don't know each other at all can have almost identical experiences. Perhaps that's why the simple phrase "me too" is so powerful. It exposes purity culture for what it is: just a script those in power read lines from to prop up the status quo while everyone else is expected to stand and applaud the performance.

When I was forced to forgive my own abuser on the very same day his behavior was exposed, I said the words to make the pain stop. I knew the sooner I said I forgave him, the sooner I would be left alone to pick up the pieces of my sanity and start collaging them back together again. But as long as I live, I will never forget that he did not say the words back to me. "I'm sorry," I uttered pathetically, my voice shaking so hard I wondered if he heard me. "I'm sorry, I'm sorry," I repeated. And on the other end of the line: silence. He never said he forgave me in return. Maybe he knew deep down that there was nothing to forgive me for. But he had also not been conditioned from birth to forgive people whenever they asked for it. He had been told he was a human being. He had been taught that his health and well-being were of the utmost importance, and people like me were responsible for ensuring he got what he deserved. He was the one who actually had something to apologize for. But I was the one forced to forgive.

I imagine a world in which no one grows up as a human giver. But the reality is that we all occupy varying identities, some of which are characterized by great privilege. We are not just women, survivors, LGBTQ. Many of us are white, middle class, literate, able bodied, educated, and comfortably housed. Utilizing *and sacrificing* the power and privilege you have for the sake of those who have less are a key part of justice work. So what might a framework for self-sacrifice look like outside the bounds of patriarchy and purity culture?

—

"Greater love has no one than this," Jesus is recorded as saying in the Gospel of John, "to lay down one's life for one's friends" (John 15:13 NIV). Survivors of sexualized violence who were abused in church may hear this as a call to sacrifice themselves for the sake of their abusers. And with good reason—it has so often been used that way against them. But

I would like to offer an alternative understanding of what it means to sacrifice oneself.

In the years since my estrangement from my biological family, I have found great comfort in other words of Jesus from the Gospel of Luke. "For those who want to save their life will lose it, and those who lose their life for my sake will save it," Jesus says in Luke 9:24. Just a few chapters later, in Luke 14, Jesus goes even further: "Whoever comes to me and does not hate father and mother, wife and children, brothers and sisters, yes, and even life itself, cannot be my disciple. Whoever does not carry the cross and follow me cannot be my disciple" (Luke 14:26–27).

One of the biggest reasons I think people struggle to extricate themselves from the shackles of purity culture is fear—fear of what their church will think, fear of what their pastor will think, fear of what their Facebook friends will think, fear of losing their lives as they know them. This fear isn't entirely unfounded. In fact, it's very reasonable. The reality is that when you no longer play the game of biblical literalism and purity culture, people take their ball and go home. They fire you, unfriend you, pretend not to see you in the grocery store, harass you online, and tell all your former friends how you've backslidden. If you change your mind, *you will lose your life*. It will never look the same again. You will lose things—people, opportunities, comfort, and perhaps even jobs or livelihood. Opening your eyes to the suffering your own theology has caused in the world is not for the faint of heart. Neither is coming forward and troubling your community's cool and calm waters by exposing a beloved member as a predator.

But on the other side, you will gain an open heart and a clear conscience. You will gain the opportunity to love like you've never loved before, in a real, up-close-and-personal way, not just from afar with a chasm of bible verses separating you from others. You will, as Jesus said, ironically end up saving your life. This, to me, is what we should talk about when we talk about self-sacrifice. Self-sacrifice is the willingness to lay down your life as it is in order to tell the truth. It is being willing to undergo a painful metamorphosis so that layers of falsehood and oppression can be finally shed. It is solidarity with the marginalized, both people who are marginalized like you and people who aren't. It is being brave even when that bravery means burning a few bridges.

Human beings versus human givers is a false dichotomy. We are all human beings, and we all must give. Survivors, your health and well-being should never be demanded of you to save someone else, especially not your abuser. That kind of "forgiveness" is cheap and meaningless, based in the power-hoarding impulse of purity culture, and it is not any kind of forgiveness worth pursuing. When and if you forgive is up to you. It is a gift you give to yourself, not a tax you pay for being abused in a Christian community. And to those who wish to be allies to survivors, I say this: those who want to save their lives will lose them. Clinging tightly to the theology that got you here will never illuminate the path forward. Loosen your grip on your life and stand in solidarity in a way that costs you something. Sit with your discomfort. Welcome it in. Take a deep breath. Kneel down. Light that bridge on fire. And walk away.

10

HEALING PATHS DIVERGE

At this point in the book, I imagine us all walking down a woodland path together. So far, we've been journeying alongside one another in excavating the evils of purity culture and learning what we must put behind us in order to be healthy and free. But up ahead is a clearing. And as we get closer, and the sun breaks through the treetops, we begin to see that it's not just a fork in our path but rather many dozens of trails that branch off from the place we're standing. We strain our eyes to see farther down each trail, and we begin to understand that from here, we will not all take the same route.

There is not only one way to be free. Rejecting this dualism, this black-and-white thinking that evangelicalism handed down as gospel truth to so many of us, is a crucial part of the process of healing. There are very few nonnegotiables, or things you absolutely *must* do to be well and to contribute to the liberation of other survivors. There's really just one big one, and it's this:

Reject, dismantle, and replace purity culture.

That's it. Full stop, no buts. We have seen how destructive and evil purity culture is and how its consequences echo in the lives of survivors, even for generations. There is no way to hold on to any part of purity culture without simultaneously being a part of the problem. Saying that you want to heal and help survivors while upholding the parts of purity culture that you feel uncomfortable letting go of is akin to saying, "I'm allergic to nuts and I'll go into anaphylactic shock if I eat them, so I'm gonna stop eating walnuts, almonds, and pistachios—but the bible says to eat hazelnuts, so those can't possibly hurt! Oh, and my pastor told me it's important to eat cashews, so I'll still eat those." The cure is not the disease. The baby and the bathwater both must go.

But purity culture is pernicious and hard to eliminate completely. Lingering purity culture often shows up in theological claims like "I believe the Bible affirms same-sex relationships, as long as they wait until marriage just like heterosexual couples," or "I think people should be able to make the sexual decisions that feel right for them whenever that is, even if they're not married! But I still believe that all romantic relationships have to be monogamous." The problem is, these statements represent *compromises* with purity culture. Purity culture doesn't just operate as the singular, disconnected ideas of sexism, homophobia, and so on. It operates as a system, and it must be dismantled as a system. If we really want to heal from the sexualized violence of purity culture and create a safer world for survivors and all marginalized groups in our communities, these half-hearted efforts will not do. Purity culture must be scraped, bit by bit, from our minds and hearts until there is nothing left of it. In the words of the apostle Paul, "make no provision" (Romans 13:14). Let it go, completely.[1]

But when it comes time to replace purity culture, the waters get a little murkier. The way is not so clear. There are lots of options, and not all of them are right for every person in every situation. Many conservative theological pundits make a career out of insinuating that the absence of purity culture means we have no sexual ethic at all. In the words of fictional character Marcia Langman of the Society for Family Stability Foundation in the television show *Parks and Recreation*, they claim that the opposite of purity culture is a "horrifying sex den where people can put their body parts anywhere they want to with impunity."[2]

But we know this simply isn't true. Everybody has a sexual ethic. It may not be yours (and it may or may not be healthy), but everybody has values that determine the sexual choices they make. In this book, I will not endeavor to lay out what I think is a "healthy sexual ethic" or a "sex-positive Christian theology," although you will find many resources in the back of this book to help you if you are wrestling with those questions. What I can do is paint a broad-strokes picture of some of the various things that #ChurchToo survivors have done and continue to do in order to facilitate their own healing and contribute to a culture that supports other survivors.

Reckoning with the Place of Christianity in Your Life

After extricating themselves completely from the controlling tendrils of purity culture, the first thing many #ChurchToo survivors have to do is reckon with what place, if any, Christianity will continue to have in their lives. Some will choose to leave Christianity altogether for either atheism, agnosticism, or another religion or spiritual practice. I want to affirm this option as good and healthy. If you are trying to figure out what you can do to help survivors while still keeping people "in the fold," you will always end up prioritizing the latter at the expense of the former. People are allowed to leave. Survivors are allowed to decide that the best option for them is to never darken the doors of a church again. Some people will find the most health and wholeness outside the bounds of the institutional church or anything that resembles "orthodox" Christian belief. We should honor, affirm, and celebrate that.

Yet other survivors will find a home in a Christian community that affirms their experiences, honors their identities, and advocates for healthy and sex-positive Christian theology. Many Christian communities are willing to do the work of becoming a safe place for survivors and healing the wounds that purity culture has inflicted in the past. They have served as safe havens for this category of survivors, allowing them to attend, serve, and lead in the context of a religion that once represented their ultimate oppression. This, too, is a legitimate approach to healing. If there is one thing I have less tolerance for than purity culture, it's the perspective that all religion is inherently evil and everyone who participates in it is either intellectually inferior or morally broken.

Still, other survivors will stay in churches and denominations that do not reject purity culture, do not make efforts to center survivors in their theology of sexuality, and show no signs of changing their minds in the immediate future. Some of these survivors may feel called to stay and change "from the inside," while others do not see any problem with purity culture and attribute the #ChurchToo crisis to a failure of policy rather than theology. My word of caution here is this: make sure you are actually making change from the inside. I know what it's like to be captivated by the fantasy that you are going to be the one to finally make things change. You are going to be the one who convinces everybody there's a problem, and they're not going to say no to you. By and large, this is a fantasy. I'm not saying change never happens. I'm saying the number of times it happens is statistically insignificant.

As I'm writing this book, a concerted online advocacy effort is underway to get Paige Patterson, the Southern Baptist leader I discussed in the previous chapter who covered up multiple cases of sexual assault and intimidated survivors into silence, disinvited from several speaking engagements he has booked. I agree that Patterson should not ever again be allowed to serve in a position of theological leadership or be considered a credible source of moral guidance. But disinviting him from speaking engagements isn't enough. He will simply be replaced with another Southern Baptist speaker or theologian, who will still teach that women should not be in pastoral leadership, homosexuality is a grave sin, and sex is to be reserved for marriage between a man and a woman only. Purity culture still forms the bedrock of the #ChurchToo crisis, no matter who it is spoken by. And change "from within" will only be effective if it is directed at purity culture itself.

I have taken somewhat of a hybrid approach on my path of healing. I still attend a church—a very small, very gay Episcopal church close to my house. I volunteer, I give, and I show up. I attend two or three Sundays out of the month. The other Sundays I sleep in, do yoga, and get mimosas at the local lesbian bar. I do not say the creeds, and I have not been confirmed, nor will I be. I work at a Presbyterian

(PCUSA) church as the administrative assistant. Monday through Friday, I'm answering phones, making bulletins, and crafting email newsletters. A couple of months after I started, the pastor took me out to lunch. "I don't know why you're here," she said, "but I'm glad you are."

"I don't know why I'm here, either," I replied. "I think I'm just trying to work my stuff out."

I've done a lot of interviews about #ChurchToo, and inevitably the interviewers always ask me whether I still identify as a Christian. I always tell them I'm bored with the question. When people ask, "Are you still a Christian?" usually what they're asking is whether or not I still ascribe to some arbitrary list of theological truth claims in order to determine whether I fall in line with "orthodoxy" or not. But that's not how I conceive of my faith. My faith is more flexible and expansive than that. My faith is based on how I behave, on the actions I take in the world, and on the values that help determine those actions. To me, Christian faith is determined by whether you find the life and actions of Jesus compelling and seek to follow in those footsteps. If you do, great. If you don't, that's fine too. But I'm deeply unconcerned about the question of whether I'm a Christian, because I don't think it's the most important thing. The most important thing is what you do in the world, not what you claim to believe or what words you use to categorize that belief. Everyone is allowed to find the path that leads to healing for them. No matter what choice survivors make, we have to make room for options both inside and outside the Christian faith.

Defining Your Sexual Values

In the wake of purity culture (which tells you there is only one right choice to make) and abuse (which attempts to steal your agency from you by force), it can be extremely difficult to reconnect with your internal self-guidance and make sexual choices based on your values rather than outside pressure. As I said before, everybody has a sexual ethic. What's yours? It's up to you to find out. You may find that the values that have been determining your sexual choices are ones you stand by, ones you're proud of and want to keep for the future. But you may also find that some of your sexual choices have sprung from values you no longer want to hold, values that developed as coping mechanisms to help you survive the trauma you experienced but that no longer help you live the kind of life you want to live. We kid ourselves if we believe that we can jump out of purity culture and into a new sexual ethic without making any mistakes or carrying any of that baggage with us into our new sexual lives. Committing mentally to a new framework is one thing, but it takes our bodies a long time—sometimes even years—to catch up. Our bodies don't always know that we're out of purity culture. We have to do the work to show them every day, understanding that it may take some time for our bodies to feel as free as we would like them to.

That work often takes the shape of small, daily decisions to honor your body and its needs in ways that your body and its needs were never honored in purity culture or by those who abused you. In purity culture, what you wanted didn't matter. Your yes and your no were essentially meaningless, because your opinion was never taken into account at all. Abusers make unilateral decisions to do things *to* you and use coercion, manipulation, and deceit to accomplish their will. So if you want to show up for your body, you have to do the opposite.

This work looks like asserting your boundaries. It looks like developing them if you don't have very many or if the boundaries you have are porous. It looks like defending and sticking up for yourself and viewing yourself as an active participant in your sexual life rather than as a person to whom things merely *happen*. It looks like acknowledging what you want—what you truly want, not just what you feel like you should want or what you think the other person wants or what you've been told to want by some outside power—and communicating that even when it's hard. Showing up for your body means prioritizing its truth and its needs, and it means learning how to find out what those things are through the weeds that have grown up around you over the years.

These steps can, of course, be very difficult to take when you have been traumatized. And this is where self-compassion becomes especially crucial, because we are not going to get it right every time. Sometimes we will let ourselves down. We will not always show up for ourselves when it counts. But as we do the work over time, our intention ought to be that we will always be growing and healing and doing better. We cannot control the past. We cannot control what happened to us. We cannot change anything that already is. But now, in this moment, we can make a different choice. We can take responsibility for what we do going forward. We can refuse to allow the script that has been written for us to be the script that determines the ending.

Purity culture is a mindfuck. Trauma rewires the brain.[3] We know this from science *and* experience. But it does not have to be the story of the rest of our lives.

Mindfulness and Movement

I remember when I was a kid, my siblings and I would obsessively watch Bob Ross on PBS every afternoon, staring at the television in the basement of our home with rapt awe as Bob created seemingly endless colorful landscapes out of blank canvases and talked about "happy trees." One day, our mother was preoccupied doing something else, so we just kept watching PBS after Bob Ross was over. And after Bob Ross came yoga. A woman came on the screen and began instructing a yoga practice for viewers at home to follow along with. We practiced with her for about ten minutes before my mother realized we never came upstairs, and when she popped her head down the stairs and saw what we were doing, she lost it. She flew down the stairs and turned off the television, ushering us back up to the kitchen while telling us that we were never, ever to watch yoga again.

I would relay this story as a funny anecdote during my own yoga teacher training program many years later. It wasn't exactly traumatizing, and I think my mother's behavior sprang less out of a fear of mindfulness and more out of a fear of anything she associated with Eastern religions (*Mulan*, for example, was the only Disney movie we were not allowed to watch). But ironically, yoga might have really helped me as a child—and it was one thing that I most definitely did not have access to.

For me, the practice of yoga as an adult has felt like a spiritual rescue mission, where I am both the one doing the saving and the one being scooped up into the net. This ancient practice has been a safe testing ground where I can learn how to do hard things.[4] Yoga teaches me how to be resilient *and* practice vulnerability and then how to take those things off the mat with me and into the world so that it changes how I actually live my life, how I move and love and work and fight and vote and grow. Teaching and practicing yoga has been one of the supreme honors of my lifetime, and not just because of how it has helped me deal with my trauma.

But oh, has it helped me deal with my trauma. I hated my body for a long time. And I don't know if I would go so far as to say that I "love" it now, but I trust it. I know I can rely on it. I know the incredible things it is capable of. I know that my body is capable of sitting in fear and discomfort and even pain and yet surviving. I know that when I feel pain, I don't have to panic. I know that just because I'm doing something now doesn't mean I need to keep doing it if it stops working. I know that I can be vulnerable and open my heart and it might actually turn out OK. I know that it is safe to be still. These are all lessons I have learned on my yoga mat.

In addition to yoga, I also run. I get on the treadmill at the gym, and I run and run until I outrun my demons and they're miles back eating my dust. During the course of writing this book, I ran over 130 miles and did a 10K race. When people ask me how I take care of myself while writing and thinking about sexual violence constantly, that is what I tell them.

But your method of mindfulness and movement doesn't have to be anything nearly as intense as hours of hot yoga and distance running—those choices aren't accessible or realistic for every person. There are so many ways to practice mindfulness and find joyful movement that allows you to inhabit your body in a safe and healing way. Some people find this healing through walking, or swimming, or chair yoga, which is done almost entirely while seated. Still others find that just sitting and practicing mindfulness meditation is what they need. I find that inhabiting my body, no matter how I am doing it, is a form of prayer. I don't pray much anymore in the evangelical sense of the word. I spend so much time every day being mindful of my thoughts and my body, I don't feel like I'm missing it.

Regardless of which method of reconnecting with the physical body you choose, the key takeaway and one of the most important lessons I have learned about trauma is this: The only people who will betray you are people who regularly, consistently betray themselves. If you don't want to be the kind of person that betrays other people, then you have to do the work of learning how not to betray yourself. And a physical or mindfulness practice of some sort is an incredible way to start doing that. It's a powerful thing to say that you are going to do something and then do it—to say that you are going to go to a certain class or run a certain number of miles or walk to a certain location and back or sit for a certain number of minutes and observe your own thoughts *and then do it.* When you keep promises to yourself, the body starts to learn to trust again. What you say is going to happen, happens. The body also learns that it is not irrelevant in the healing process—that it must be taken into account and that its needs and feelings are important.

No one has to do any one particular kind of physical or mindfulness practice. I've shared what has worked for me, and you get to decide what works for you. But the body and its connection to the mind cannot be ignored or cast to the side. *Especially* for survivors who grew up in a culture that demonized that body and viewed it as the source of all sin and evil, reconnecting with the body in a way that works for you is key. Many of us grew up, to quote Paul in 1 Corinthians, beating our bodies and making them our slaves and being told that our ability to do so was proof we were holy. We must unlearn those lessons, not if we are to be holy, but if we are to be whole.

A final word of caution: In *The Body Keeps the Score*, Dr. Bessel Van Der Kolk notes that "after trauma the world is experienced with a different nervous system that has an altered perception of risk and safety. . . . Trauma has shut down their inner compass."[5] Sometimes a traumatized body may tell you to panic when you're safe. Sometimes a traumatized body may tell you to lie to or run from the people who love you. Maybe it will tell you to not put any vegetables in your body for days at a time or to hook up with that person who is terrible for your mental health. My suggestion for navigating this tension isn't that we "listen to the body" less but rather that we expand our definition of what it means to listen. Listening to the body doesn't mean uncritically following all its impulses. Listening can mean acknowledging and still making a different choice that is rooted in your values. The body almost never lies, but the traumatized body is not always operating at 100 percent when it comes to perceiving the truth. Part of the healing process is learning how to differentiate the aftershocks of trauma from the communications of a body that is finely tuned by evolution to know exactly what it wants and needs. This might require calling on additional help, which brings me to my next point.

Therapy and Medication

First, let me start by saying that I am aware that therapy is, unfortunately, a privilege in the United States. It is not feasible for everybody for a myriad of reasons, including high cost as well as lack of access to religiously competent, LGBTQ-affirming, and sex-positive therapists. In the appendix in the back of this book, you'll find information about several therapists and therapy collectives who meet those criteria, as well as a list of suggestions for finding affordable and trustworthy therapists in your area. I myself see a sliding scale therapist. You may find this shocking, but writing about why the institutional evangelical church is wrong about sex is not a particularly lucrative career path, and I'm all too familiar with the way that accessing mental health care sometimes feels like forging your own path through the forest with a machete.

With that being said, quality mental health care is a crucial part of healing for survivors in the wake of purity culture–saturated abuse, and I would encourage everyone who can seek help to do so. The first time I stumbled into my therapist's office on a hot Nashville afternoon in August, I was twenty-five years old, in the beginning stages of being disowned by my biological family, and had just come out to my then husband after being married for a little over a year. Over the years, I had shared the story of my abuse with close friends, but for the first time, I had as many sessions as I needed to talk about what had happened to me. Within a month, I stood up to my parents for the final time and confronted them about their failure to protect me when I was taken advantage of a decade before. A couple of months after that, I began speaking up about my sexuality online, even though it would have been less complicated to let people assume I was straight because of my marriage. A year later, #ChurchToo was born.

Going to therapy was like pulling a piece of shrapnel out of my body. It needed to happen, but the bleeding was going to get worse before it got better. The elation of finally tasting freedom was quickly replaced with a fundamental sense of terror at not knowing what to do with it. Now that it was OK for me to be who I was, I had to figure out who the fuck

I was. My marriage started to crumble as I began to understand that I was gay. I tried desperately to hold it together, with duct tape and staples and a fervent prayer, but nothing was working. I had been waiting and waiting for my family to come back, to apologize, to say they were sorry and invite me to Christmas, and they never did. I was sinking deeper and deeper into depression. At a certain point, I dropped every plate I was spinning and watched them all shatter into a million pieces in front of me in slow motion.

I had my first (diagnosed) bipolar manic episode in July 2018, eight months after I first shared my #ChurchToo story. I get asked a lot about how I manage to do this work and maintain my mental health. And the truth is, at times I haven't. I know what to look for now, my own personal red flags, but I didn't then. As I came down from the manic high in the days that followed the worst of it, I went crawling back to my therapist's office, in the same run-down building in which I'd first seen her, with the same black-eyed Susans blooming in the planter outside. I talked for the entirety of our hour together, and she referred me to a psychiatrist immediately. Within a week, my new psychiatrist, a drummer with a side obsession with yoga and bodywork, had diagnosed me with bipolar and started me on medication.

I'd love to say everything has been perfect since then, that I just got on medication and kept going to therapy and it fixed everything and there have been no lasting repercussions from the "cornucopia of trauma"[6] I've endured. But it's not true. I had another manic episode. I had it while writing this book. I had it while taking my medication religiously. It wasn't as bad as the first one, but it was still bad. I'll probably have another one. I'll likely keep having them the rest of my life from time to time, and there's probably not much I can do to change that, not with all the yoga and running and green smoothies and therapy and lithium in the world. It's a thing I have to live with because of what I've gone through.

Not everyone who is a survivor of sexualized violence has a mental illness. But sexualized violence has long-lasting, far-reaching detrimental effects on mental health, a fact that has been proven by multiple studies. One study found that 80 percent of teenage girls who had been sexually assaulted suffered from anxiety, depression, posttraumatic stress disorder (PTSD), or other serious health conditions in the months following their assault—and 55 percent suffered from two of those conditions.[7] The Rape, Abuse and Incest National Network (RAINN) reports that "33% of women who are raped contemplate suicide" and that people who have been sexually assaulted are more likely to struggle with drug addiction, as they are six times more likely to use cocaine and ten times more likely to use other hard drugs.[8] Just in my own circle of friends and acquaintances, I know survivors of sexualized violence, abuse, assault, and rape who live with bipolar disorder, borderline personality disorder, PTSD, eating disorders, depression, anxiety, obsessive-compulsive disorder, substance use and abuse issues, and more.

People who uphold purity culture need to come face-to-face with what they are actually advocating for—a culture of mental health issues stemming directly from their theology and the abuses their theology sustains. Even those who haven't directly experienced abuse in the church but grew up in purity culture are more prone to struggle with their mental health. The whole system *is* sexualized violence, and when people make it out alive with their mental health intact, that is a miracle, not an expected result—and it is usually a miracle facilitated by a great deal of privilege.

But regardless of the precise type of sexualized violence you've experienced, asking for professional help as you're able and opening yourself up to the possibility of medical intervention is a path worth exploring for many people. It's hard to do the first time, but there is no shame in asking for help. Acknowledging that your body reacted to your trauma in particular somatic, psychological, and chemical ways that may present as mental illnesses or disorders in order to protect you can be an opportunity to practice *gratitude* toward your mind and body as you figure out what to do next and how to be healthy moving forward. Everyone needs help sometimes, and sometimes that help takes the form of a weighted blanket in a therapist's office and a little pink pill two times a day.

—

On a Sunday afternoon in early February, I went to a local vegan restaurant in Nashville to meet up with my friend Laura, a psychotherapist who specializes in religious trauma. I like Laura because she likes to talk about all the same kinds of things I like to talk about and also because she is as big of a *Bachelor* franchise fanatic as I am and has been a guest on the *Reality Steve Podcast*, a personal and professional fantasy of mine. I grazed on my salad as I told her what I was writing about, and I asked her what she thought about survivors of sexualized violence in churches trying to reckon with the place that Christianity—the religion that wrought so much harm in their minds and bodies—should have in their lives going forward.

"Well, first of all," Laura said, "I'm not antichurch, or antireligion. But I'm very antipower, -control, -abuse, and

-harm. Oftentimes it does help a survivor to step away from traditional religious practices, at least for a little bit. Not forever, but just to give you a break from entering into those potentially abusive situations. It's very hard to heal from something when you're still in it. We have to wait for the crisis to be over in order to grieve and heal." I nodded, thinking of how I'd stopped going to church for a while in my early deconstruction after the third or fourth time I'd walked out of a service I'd been invited to by friends. I made my way back when I was good and ready, and it wasn't to a church where an all-male pastoral staff stood onstage and delivered homophobic sermons in a tone that suggested they were deeply apologetic for being the bearers of the bad news that the kingdom of God did not include queer folks.

"When you take that break," Laura continued, "it gives you the safety and the opportunity to ask what you would want spirituality and religion to look like, and if there's somewhere in the middle where you can define who God is to you, or if you want these practices in your life at all."

"It's easier said than done," I observed.

"Oh, absolutely," she said. "The way that trauma and abuse work is that our brain has messages coming in, and when they're repeated over and over and over, they become neurologically wired into our brain. And that wiring sends chemical messages down to our body that makes us have physiological and psychological responses." That's why it's so much harder to get your body on board with a change, even after you've made up your mind to do or believe something different, Laura explained. "Essentially, even though I no longer consciously believe this thing, whether it's purity culture or something else, it's not uncommon that when I go to do that thing, my body has a different response than my mind. While changing our beliefs is a start, the work that we have to do to remove the trauma response and the physiological response comes on a body-based level."

Laura noted that when she works with clients who've experienced trauma—particularly religious trauma—she finds body-based practices like yoga, mindfulness, and eye movement desensitization and reprocessing (EMDR) especially helpful. "We *have* to process trauma through the body," she said. "It's by going back into our bodies that we're able to release the energy from our trauma, and then we don't carry it anymore."

"When you look at purity culture," Laura told me, "the message of divorcing your body is huge. We are taught messages like your body is evil, you need to make it your slave, and so on. And that's also a common side effect of any sort of abuse. So it's getting back to your body and finding safety in your body that's important, because the message that your body is evil also means that your body isn't safe. Building that relationship with your body is so key and transformative because we have to be able to feel like our bodies are safe. In my opinion, it's not until that safety is built that progress can happen."

I started to ask Laura about building your own sexual ethic in the wake of purity culture, but I suddenly realized the answer to that question was probably almost identical to the answer to the question of how to healthily reintegrate religion into your life after abuse (if that's something you want to do).

"Patriarchy is built on a dynamic of power and control," Laura said. "When we look at reintegrating religion back in, it's built on choice and autonomy and individuality.

Key questions are, Do I have the ability to choose? Can I be different from this group that I'm a part of and still be accepted? Can I change my beliefs? Can I ask questions?"

"It's the same with sex," I replied, finishing the thought.

"Right," she said. "Is there choice? Is there autonomy? Is there individuality? The other important thing if you want to construct a sexual ethic based on your values is that you have to figure out what your values are. Values can be fluid. It's important to give yourself a lot of space and take away the rigidity and ask, What does this look like for me *right now* in this season of my life? What does sex mean to me, and what do I want it to mean?"

I mused that learning to define and refine your sexual ethic like that requires a good grasp on boundaries. "Do you find that people who have come out of purity culture or experienced sexual abuse have a difficult time holding boundaries?" I asked her.

"Definitely. When it comes to purity culture and sexual abuse—and purity culture is sexual abuse," Laura said, "it's a bulldozing of anything that you want. Choice and autonomy are taken away. It's others telling you what they're going to do, and you don't get a choice. So we start to learn that it doesn't actually matter what we want and that our desires, our thoughts, and our bodies don't matter."

"You're basically quoting a whole chapter of my book," I laughed.

She smiled. "So that's something that's very important when we look at healing from purity culture and abuse," she said. "You have to ask yourself what healthy boundaries look like to you so that you can navigate relationships in a way that feels healthy."

"So how exactly do you define religious trauma?" I asked her.

Laura pulled out her phone and read from an Instagram post on her profile, where she educates people about trauma, therapy, boundaries, and healing: "Religious trauma is the physical, emotional, or psychological response to religious beliefs, practices, or structures that overwhelm an individual's ability to cope and return to a sense of safety. So . . ." She paused, thinking. "In order to understand religious trauma, you have to understand trauma. 'Religious' is just an adjective. Trauma is our body's physiological response to an overwhelming event. It's subjective, it's perceptive, it's embodied, and it's subconscious."

Sometimes, we mistake trauma for the thing itself that happened to us or the series of things we had to endure. But trauma isn't the actual event; it's what our body does *in response to* the event. When the body becomes overwhelmed, it has to fight, flight, freeze, or fawn in order to cope with the sensations and survive the situation. And when we aren't able to release that overwhelming energy—when we're forced to bottle it up inside or when we don't have the coping skills to dispel it—that's how you get trauma.

Laura told me that purity culture fits the clinical definition of a complex trauma. And that trauma impacts our physiology—sometimes permanently. "Especially when we look at things like bipolar," Laura gestured across the table at me, "or autoimmune disorders, it's like—it *could* be reversed. It is possible. There's a significant amount of research that indicates that processing trauma can sometimes help autoimmune disorders or other mental and physical health issues reverse themselves. But that's not a guarantee. What we've endured can literally have permanent effects."

I sighed, exhaling a quiet laugh. I told Laura about how I had a manic episode while I was writing this book, about how I was doing all the things like yoga and running and therapy and it still wasn't enough sometimes, about how I might just have to live with this forever because that's what my body did to try to help me survive, and about how I was trying to practice gratitude toward my body, but it is hard when it feels like it's trying to kill me. She smiled and nodded knowingly.

One thing Laura said stuck with me: "Reconstruction is part of trauma work." We can't replace something with nothing. We have to ask ourselves what we want our lives to look like now—what we want our relationships and our boundaries to look like. We have to do the work of determining how we want our relationship to God and spirituality to look as well as our relationship to sex and sexuality. We have to learn the skills we need to deal with the trauma we have already experienced and, hopefully, reduce instances of further traumatization in the future. This is all proactive. It is additive. It is positive. Reconstruction is part of trauma work.

And trauma work is a job we did not ask for. We did not fill out an application or interview for the position. Most of us would probably abdicate responsibility if we could. But nonetheless, it is *our* work. And it is sacred. We cannot choose not to have the job any more than we could choose not to have blue eyes or not to have been born on our birthday. Forces so much bigger than us brought us to this moment. But we can choose how we approach the work, and we can choose how we move forward. The story is not over. It is being written anew, by us, every day that we wake up.

CONCLUSION

A couple of days after #ChurchToo first started going viral, my Facebook Messenger app dinged, and I saw the name of my best guy friend from high school light up on my phone. He had helped me through the crisis of being blamed for my abuse, and that winter he often picked me up and took me places when my parents forbade me from driving as part of my punishment. But he also remained friends with my abuser during that time, and he and I had fallen out of touch while I was in college.

I opened his message, thinking that it would be something encouraging. Several old friends from high school had reached out during those initial days, letting me know that they had no idea what had really gone on when my abuser left the church but that they were so sorry and they believed me. It had been uplifting. But instead, when I opened up his message, I read this: "He doesn't deserve this. He doesn't deserve to be called out as an abuser in front of the world with no hope or chance for discussion or forgiveness or reconciliation. . . . What he did was wrong. What he did was stupid beyond belief. What he did, and what he caused to happen, may never heal, may never be forgiven. But that doesn't make this right."

And that is how I learned that even if you have the truth on your side, there will always be some people for whom the truth is not enough.

When you finally learn how to stand on your own holy, sacred ground, not everyone will be thrilled about that—especially the people who benefit from your self-flagellation, your lack of self-esteem, your porous boundaries, and your willingness to stay silent. Some people in your story have constructed their identities around the idea that they are "good people" who have made "the right decisions" in life, and telling the truth about what actually happened will challenge those identities, make them rethink their decisions, and wonder if they've really been so good after all.

This goes for institutions as well as individuals. I truly believe that the sheer volume of vitriolic reactions to #ChurchToo from people who identify as Christians comes in part because people have constructed their identities around the church and around this (often false) idea that their church represents the "good guys," those doing right in the world and standing up for the truth and fighting evil. When they come face-to-face with direct, incontrovertible evidence to the contrary, *they literally cannot deal*, and they go on the offensive—because if what we're saying is right, then everything that gives them security and meaning in this world is built on a lie. That can't possibly be. So we survivors must be the Jezebels trying to destroy the church because of the bitterness in our hearts that makes us unwilling to forgive and come back to the fold. To see things any other way would cause too much cognitive dissonance.

Although Anne Lamott is a white woman who continues to wear her hair in locs despite people of color telling us for decades not to, she was still extremely correct when she said, "You own everything that happened to you. Tell your stories. If people wanted you to write warmly about them, they should've behaved better."[1] I cannot recommend adopting this attitude more highly. We all know that just because something is true does not technically make it worth saying. If you hate a sweater your best friend got you for your birthday, you might not want to say that. If we have an interpersonal conflict with someone we know, we don't always necessarily want to broadcast the details of the conflict to everyone on the internet. But abuse does not fall into either of those categories. If the people who abused you and the people who enabled them to do so or blamed you for being abused wanted you to write warmly about them, then, as Lamott says, they should have behaved better, and you should be free to shout your story from the mountaintops.

Often, family loyalty is weaponized to keep survivors silent in just this way. Blood is thicker than water, they say, and love means not disrupting the peace years later. But the reality is that if your family abused you or enabled your abuse or blamed you for your abuse, *they already betrayed you long ago.* There is no further betrayal you can perpetrate by being honest now. It's like trying to quit a job when you've already been fired. Some people will interpret honesty as betrayal, but that is a matter of perception, and it doesn't make it so. You are not responsible for anyone else's negative feelings about your disclosure of abuse, and it's important to cultivate those boundaries discussed in chapter 10 so that when someone tries to hand you their baggage about your life, you can push it away gently and say, "No, thanks. That doesn't belong to me."

Ultimately, the response of others to your #ChurchToo story is a reflection of *their* story, *their* experience. And while those responses may not be healthy or reflect reality, it can help if you think of them as *reasonable.* Their response makes logical sense given where they're coming from and their prior ideological commitments that—they believe—cannot be questioned without risking eternal conscious torment. It makes *sense* that people committed to the preservation of the evangelical Christian church would bristle at credible and well-placed criticism of it. It makes *sense* that people who believe that women are human givers and moral children[2] would then turn around and dismiss a movement primarily led by women, especially when that movement has a bone to pick with their favorite institution. It makes *sense* that people who think sexual shame is a virtue would deride survivors who dare to cast off the shackles of shame and stand in their truth.

Radical Acceptance

When I first got diagnosed with bipolar, my therapist had me read a workbook about something called dialectical behavior therapy (DBT). One of the main pillars of DBT is the concept of "radical acceptance." Radical acceptance says that everything about the present moment is exactly as it "should" be—not morally, but logically: "To radically accept the present moment means that you must acknowledge that the present moment is what it is due to a long chain of events and decisions made by you and other people in the past. The present moment never spontaneously leaps into existence without being caused by events that have already taken place."[3]

I had always hated "acceptance" language, but radical acceptance finally helped it make sense to me. I don't have to accept that it was OK for my abuser to prey on me or my parents to blame me. I certainly don't have to accept any moral culpability. But I do have to accept that those things *happened*, and they happened very reasonably if you consider the context. My abuser preyed on me because the church we were a part of had no structural accountability system to speak of and because I was precocious and naive and zealous for the god of evangelical Christianity, so I was chum in the water. My parents blamed me because their sexual ethics were steeped in purity culture and they had no understanding of consent and because to view me as the victim in the situation would probably have caused them to have to rethink the ethics of the genesis of their own relationship. The church swept it under the rug because it would have been much more difficult to explain to every parent in that very large youth group why a predator had unfettered access to their children for *years*.

None of this is right. But it all makes sense.

Maybe you can try this exercise. *A* happened because *B*. *C* happened because *D*. It does *not* mean that you accept or justify the unjust things that have happened to you or to others. "Radically accepting something doesn't mean that you give up and simply accept every bad situation that happens to you," the authors of the book my therapist gave me write[4]—it just means you stop trying to change what's already happened, because it's impossible. You can change the future through your choices, but you cannot change anything if you do not acknowledge how things already are. Similar to how it is important to get a correct diagnosis when you go to the doctor so that the doctor can prescribe an effective treatment, you cannot make the choices to create a different future if you are unwilling to recognize the past or the present. Katonah yoga teaches that we have to orient ourselves in the present moment in order to figure out where we are going. These are all different ways of saying the same thing.

You also can't change a situation by trying to change other people. You simply can't. You can't change anybody's past or present actions toward you, and trying to do so only sets you up for a lifetime of pain and disappointment. The only person you can change is you. The only person whose decisions you are in charge of is you. This is the baseline assumption of the concept of consent, and it applies not just to the bedroom but to all of life. You did not do anything to deserve your abuse or to put yourself in a situation to endure it. That is 100 percent on other people, who should have behaved better and *not been predators* no matter what you did.

The important thing now is to open your eyes, take a good long look at your life, and know that from here on out, you have the power to make choices to create a life that does not traumatize you—a life that brings you joy. You can develop your coping skills so that when difficult things do happen, as they inevitably will, you will know what steps to take in order to not carry them with you forever. You still have the time—it is never too late. You get to decide how you feel about God and sex and your body and the rest of your life, and nobody can stop you.

We will all take different paths from here. And that is good. We reject the fundamentalist mindset that says that for any given question, there are only "good" and "bad," "right" and "wrong" answers. This is not the end. Our paths will cross again. We will not live in shame forever, and we will make decisions we are proud of. We will mess up, and we will do better. We will learn resilience. We will learn to be human and to be OK with it. We will allow others to be human too. We will find our safe people, people that make us feel like our hearts just woke up from a lazy Saturday afternoon nap in the sun. We will learn to love our boundaries more than we love making others happy, and we will learn to take down our walls when the time is right. Mostly, we will learn to love ourselves so hard that other people not loving us will have nothing to do with how we feel about ourselves or about the work we have to do in this world.

I am ready. I have been ready. There are so many of us walking this road together. And I have faith that we will all find our way.

A Love Letter to Survivors

As I interviewed all the lovely, kind, brave, thoughtful humans that I spoke to for this book, I asked them one question at the end of our time together: "What do you have to say to survivors?"

Most of the time when I asked them that question, their faces visibly shifted, and they fell silent. A few of them started crying as they began to formulate their thoughts. I'm going to close by sharing their answers, because a conversation about abuse centered around anything other than the voices and thoughts and experiences of survivors will always ring hollow. As you read their words, you'll notice many common threads and many unique ones as well. I hope every survivor reading this book will receive these words with as much love and tenderness and courage as they were offered.

—

You're valuable. You are more important than the values that your church teaches you. Your story is more important. Your personhood is more important than what you're taught is right and wrong. It's safe to come forward. It's safe to tell your story. I've had questions about whether it was worth it or not. But as hard as it's been, you are believed. You are loved. You're treasured. You're valued. And it's safe to tell your story.

—Kenny, chapter 6

You matter. Your experience matters, and you're valid. That makes me really emotional because in religion, we're taught to hate ourselves so much. And we're taught that we don't matter. But you matter, and your experience matters, and it's OK to spend time and money and resources to work this out. There is hope in this whole process. Life isn't gonna be like this forever. It takes work, and not that there's ever an ending point, but there is life outside of this. And it's beautiful and wonderful, and you're strong and you can get through it. And the sheer fact that you're wanting to tackle it speaks so much to your courage and your strength and your capability.

—Laura, chapter 10

Keep going. It gets better.

—Julia, chapter 5

For so long, I felt so alone. I felt like I was the only person who had ever experienced anything like this. And I felt so ashamed, like, Why can I not just get over this? So I know it sounds like a bullshit answer, but God, you are not alone. And it wasn't your fault. . . . But that's a hard thing for people who have been abused in the church to understand. You're not alone; it wasn't your fault. You matter. Your story matters. When you decide to go public and name names and let go of that guilt and shame you've carried for so long, you are in control of the narrative now. And no matter how anybody reacts—your abuser, the media, whatever—you've now released that burden.

—Jules, chapter 9

I see you. I hear you. I acknowledge you. I believe you. What happened to you was wrong, and it was not your fault, and God, if you choose to believe in a higher power, is pissed about your sexual violation, and so am I.

—Lyvonne, chapter 8

What happened to you is not your fault. You're not alone; there are many people who have experienced what you've been through. Healing and recovery are possible; it's a lot of work, but it's worth it. Take all the time you need to come back to yourself. You have the right to set boundaries and do whatever you need to protect yourself. You have inherent worth and value, and nothing can diminish that. It's OK to trust yourself.

—Charlotte, chapter 2

God never meant for you to feel shame toward/in/with the body and sexuality they created for you to know how beloved you are.

—Tina, chapter 3

For me, it always comes down to love and empathy. I always quote this line from the Pink Floyd song "Echoes." So the thing I would say would be to share my favorite lyric: "If a stranger's passing in the street / by chance your separate glances meet / and I am you / and what I see is me." And that is a lyric about walking a mile in each other's shoes. Even though we're strangers, I see you and I believe you and I'm with you.

—Michael, chapter 6

And lastly, from me:

When you are in the world where your abuse occurred—the world of pain and oppression and abandonment—it feels like that is the only world there is. But the truth is this: that world is a snow globe. It's small and deceiving, and you can shatter it. And there is so much space on the outside. As the poet Nayyirah Waheed says, "There is more extraordinary love, more love that you have never seen, out here in this wide and wild universe." There is so much love and belonging and happiness and pleasure that you cannot even begin to imagine because it will take forms you will never see coming. Always remember there is more—and remember, even if all of your conditioning tells you otherwise, that you do actually deserve it.

ACKNOWLEDGMENTS

I could never write a book about sexualized violence in the twentieth and twenty-first centuries without acknowledging and thanking Tarana Burke, the many voices of the #MeToo movement, and every survivor who has come forward during this era to form the groundswell of truth that cannot now be ignored. As I said in my original tweet on the day #ChurchToo began, this is me standing on your shoulders. *There would be no #ChurchToo without #MeToo.* I felt #ChurchToo deserved its own conversation in part because some of the *reasons* that sexual abuse happens in faith communities and some of the *methods* by which it is perpetuated, justified, and explained away are so unique to those institutions. But the fact that we even get to have this conversation in this way at all is a privilege afforded to us by the people who have been doing this work since many of us were too young to understand it was even necessary—primarily other women, and especially women of color. A portion of my profit from this book will be donated to the Me Too Movement (www.metoomvmt.org) in perpetuity.

Thank you to Lisa, my editor, for telling me when I was selling myself short and challenging me to greater clarity, as well as the entire team at Broadleaf Books for helping me manifest a dream that has been in my heart my entire life—my first book.

Thank you to my fiancée, Caitlin, for the many hours spent talking through the manuscript with me and for your expert advice (most of which I actually took), your sociological prowess, your back rubs, your drink refills, your JSTOR access, and your unwavering support. Thank you for picking me up off the floor when it got to be too much. Thank you for making me feel smart and capable. I cannot wait to marry you.

Thank you to my future mother-in-law for leveraging your lifetime church lady status to get me behind the *Christianity Today* paywall.

Thank you to my therapist, who helped me create the courage to stand up for myself in so many big and small ways.

Thank you to Charlotte, Megan, Lyvonne, Julia, Kenny, Michael, Jules, Laura, Stephanie, Hilary, and Dr. Tina Schermer Sellers—this book would not be what it is without your contributions, and I am forever grateful that you allowed me to interview you. Thank you as well to all the many hundreds of humans who sent me their stories and responded to my inquiries with bravery and vulnerability. It is because of you that I am able to do this work.

Thank you to those who have been with me since I was a scared twenty-one-year-old spitting Christian spoken-word poetry in dimly lit bars in Chicago and blogging about my first kiss. It has been an honor to evolve alongside you.

Lastly, it also bears noting that during the editing process of this book, my house was hit by a deadly tornado while we were inside of it and rendered uninhabitable. Rather than that dealing a fatal blow to this book, I was able to get back up on my feet with relative quickness and complete all my edits on time, even early. This was entirely because of the generosity and compassion of the people who sent us monetary donations, helped us move and store our belongings, and opened their homes to us while we were waiting to move into our new home. Although it was a traumatic experience, I felt loved and cared for and safe enough to do the work I needed to do from start to finish because of the support of these incredible people. Special thanks to Reid, Blake, Bethany, Matt, Turner, Iman, Jeff and Mary, and the staff and community of St. Ann's Episcopal Church and Second Presbyterian Church in Nashville.

APPENDIX: FREQUENTLY ASKED QUESTIONS AND RESOURCES

I've done my best in this section to include some of the most common questions I'm asked, along with brief answers. I've also combined frequently asked questions with resources so that if there is a question you need an answer for or want to explore further, you will have several options for books, websites, and so on that can help you as you seek to expand your horizons, learn more, and help those around you.

—

I'm a pastor / youth pastor / youth leader / parent. How do I talk to my kids about sex in a way that doesn't induce shame? Is there any way for me to teach them to be abstinent until marriage without falling into the pitfalls of purity culture?

In short, no. There is no way to teach children or young adults to be abstinent until marriage without effectually teaching purity culture. However, there are lots of ways to talk to children and young adults about sex that do not induce shame and do not promote purity culture.

The Our Whole Lives (OWL) curriculum is something I cannot recommend more highly. The OWL curriculum runs from infants to elderly folks and focuses on healthy sexuality in every stage of life. You can find out more about it at https://www.uua.org/re/owl. Our Whole Lives approaches the topic of sexuality from the perspective that it is a net good for younger people to delay sexual activity but also from the perspective that sex is fundamentally good and should be celebrated.

Another good resource to share with the young people you minister to or have influence with is Scarleteen.com. Scarleteen is an independent, feminist, grassroots sexuality and relationships education media and support organization and website. Scarleteen operates from a shame-free perspective and gives honest answers to all the questions you've thought of and all the ones you haven't. They have a keyword-searchable database.

When you're looking at curriculum and speakers, make sure you don't fall for sneaky marketing. Many speakers and conferences that market themselves as "cool" and "open" places for youth to ask questions about sex are really just abstinence-only, purity-pledge outfits in disguise. As a parent or youth leader, you must be critical about the kinds of information you bring to your young people and make sure that it is not actually *dis*information. Exposing kids to different viewpoints? Good. Exposing them to lies presented as the truth? Really bad and potentially deadly. Do your research, and don't be afraid to correct course if needed. Parents especially should not be shy about advocating with their children's pastors and youth leaders to make sure that comprehensive, age-appropriate, and consent-based sexuality education is the cornerstone of any "talks" or "series" about dating, love, or relationships that may happen at church. If your church isn't willing to help equip your children in this way, uses scare tactics in order to elicit a certain reaction from your children, or is only willing to share partial or inaccurate information about sex and their bodies with them, ask them why—and consider that you may need to find a community that more closely aligns with your values.

Overall, the important thing to remember is that children and young adults are people, blessed with the same autonomy and right to self-determination that we all are. You may be able to terrorize them into submission temporarily, but you can never truly control them. Parents, pastors, and youth leaders need to do the internal work of learning to let go of the results so that they are more able to freely teach a theology of sexuality that is healthy, consistent, and informed by modern science and medicine—rather than by fear and someone's outdated interpretation of the bible.

What about Romans 1:26–27 / 1 Corinthians 6:9 / Leviticus 18:22?

Many people have lots of questions about "what the bible really says about homosexuality." When it comes to exegeting and interpreting these and other "clobber verses," I recommend the following resources in particular:

- *A Lily among the Thorns: Imagining a New Christian Sexuality* and *Liberating Sexuality: Justice between the Sheets* by Miguel A. De La Torre
- *God and the Gay Christian: The Biblical Case in Support of Same-Sex Relationships* by Matthew Vines
- Matthew Vines's hour-long YouTube video "The Bible and Homosexuality," available at https://www.youtube.com/watch?v=ezQjNJUSraY

- The resources from the Metropolitan Community Church, which can be found at https://www .mccchurch.org/resources/mcc-theologies/

Many others have written about this topic, but I think these resources address the question most directly. However, it should be noted that out of all the options listed above, only the Metropolitan Community Church is officially supportive of nonmonogamous relationships, and Vines is not supportive of premarital sex either (though De La Torre is). Vines officially teaches that LGBTQ relationships that are monogamous and abstinent before marriage are supported by Scripture, and De La Torre writes that nonmonogamous relationships can never be truly safe. I think both of those positions fail to do Scripture and LGBTQ persons justice. However, Vines and De La Torre are still very good resources when it comes to dealing with the biblical text itself, especially if you are having conversations with people for whom "what the bible says" is the only thing that matters when determining the morality of a given action. Vines and De La Torre are both adept at showing that these verses that have so often been used to keep LGBTQ persons in bondage do not actually mean what they are purported to mean and that the exegetical evidence supporting their "traditional" interpretation is specious at best. If you're a person who would like to be affirming but feels held back by your interpretation of the bible, I strongly suggest that you avail yourself of these resources.

If you don't agree with purity culture, is your sexual ethic just "anything goes"?

I don't think there's a single person out there who truly has an "anything goes" sexual ethic. Everyone has a sexual ethic—Christians, atheists, straight people, LGBTQ people, monogamous people, polyamorous people—and none of them believe every sexual act is completely ethical at all times. "Anything goes" tends to just be a boogeyman, a placeholder onto which people can project their fears and insecurities even though no one actually operates their sexual ethics in that way.

There is a veritable chasm between "sex is only for a man and a woman in the context of a legal, monogamous, lifelong marriage" and "anything goes." Trying to pretend that those are the only two options is intellectually dishonest, as is painting consent as some kind of "Get Out of Jail Free" card that covers over a multitude of other sins.

If you're someone who is in the process of deconstructing purity culture yourself and you're looking for help in learning how to define your boundaries and (re)construct your sexual ethic, I highly recommend checking out licensed mental health counselor Matthias Roberts's book *Beyond Shame: Creating a Healthy Sex Life on Your Own Terms*. Roberts does an amazing job compassionately engaging with hard questions and meeting people where they're at in order to help move them toward a healthier place.

How can my church avoid having a #ChurchToo problem? What do churches have to do in order to respond to abuse appropriately and care well for survivors?

There are two aspects to this question: prevention and response. Most churches that are deeply committed to purity culture, like the Southern Baptist Convention, focus solely on the response. They are reacting (poorly) to instance after instance of sexual abuse in their midst, and they will keep having to do so for the foreseeable future because none of their actions are contributing to the project of prevention.

On the one hand, it is impossible to prevent 100 percent of abuse. Predators are skilled at deceit and manipulation, and as many have rightly pointed out, sexual violence is found in all kinds of churches and outside of church walls in politics, pop culture, other religions, and our own families. But on the other hand, if you know what to look for, it is certainly possible sometimes to stop abuse before it occurs or before it escalates.

There are many different abuse prevention training programs. I have personally taken two: one for employment purposes and another when I was a Sunday school teacher in the Episcopal church. Your particular church or denomination may have its own program. If it doesn't, you should ask why. These programs will usually focus on helping to increase your awareness of people who regularly "break rules" or push established boundaries with children or vulnerable people, since this is usually the first step in grooming.

For churches that are interested in working with an organization, I highly recommend reaching out to Stephanie and Hilary from Into Account, whom I interviewed in chapter 5. They also have a comprehensive checklist for churches that

I mentioned, which covers everything from mandatory reporting laws to survivor advocacy and beyond—and it also focuses on cultural prevention, or creating a community that is hostile to predators, who are often attracted to environments where sexual shame rules. Their website is intoaccount.org.

The best thing you can do to care well for survivors in your church is to do everything in your power to help your church divest from purity culture and form a robust theology of sexuality that is sex positive and consent based. Recognize that adding more sexual shame onto the dumpster fire of shame survivors are probably already feeling will never be the answer. If you want to be a true ally, think less of how uncomfortable it makes you to rethink your theology of sexuality and more of how you can wield your privilege to make the world a less horrific place for people who have been harmed by that theology.

I'm a student on a Christian college campus where we have to follow purity culture or we risk being kicked out. Are there any resources for me?

Check out Soulforce. They focus on the LGBTQ community, but their mission is to end the religious oppression of all marginalized communities through nonviolent resistance, and they do a lot of work on college campuses. Depending on how aggressive your college's stance is, there may be clubs or affinity groups you can join at varying levels of visibility to the administration. Q Christian Fellowship (formerly Gay Christian Network) does a great job of bringing Christian young people together for community and information-sharing, and although that organization is also focused on LGBTQ persons, faith-based LGBTQ organizations are good places to start because they are already doing the work of unlearning the traditional, "biblical" understanding of sex and sexuality.

Also, never underestimate the importance of your local Planned Parenthood. They will have free or cheap condoms and other single-use contraceptives, and you'll be able to talk confidentially to a health professional about sex if you need to. They can also help you get access to various birth control options or long-acting reversible contraceptives like the IUD. And most importantly, you can get accurate *information*—even if your college won't give it to you. Always remember that Scarleteen.com is available too. You may have to log off your campus Wi-Fi in order to access their site, since some Christian colleges filter out sex educations sites, but you can use your smartphone if you have one or head to your local library to use the computers there.

Make sure to reach out online for community regardless. There are likely other people on your college campus going through the same struggle, but even if there aren't, I guarantee you there is someone (and probably a lot of someones) online who gets it. Twitter is a good place to start because you can connect with a lot of people quickly (hashtags like #ChurchToo and #PurityCulture can get you started), but there are also forums, group chats, and private Facebook groups. Just always look out for the "but" when looking for online community: "We love you, *but* your sexuality is still sinful according to the Bible"; "We affirm your dream of being a woman pastor, *but* you have to be a cisgender woman"; "Purity culture hurts people, *but* sex should still be saved for marriage." The "buts" always tell the difference between a group that is serious about change and a group that is merely rebranding or repackaging purity culture. It takes a little digging, but you can find community with people who understand what it's like to be on a Christian college campus having purity culture shoved down your throat. And hopefully, you can support each other as you try to survive and thrive in that environment.

I grew up in purity culture, and I struggle with sexual shame and knowledge about my own body. How can I start learning more accurate information about sex?

Undertaking the work of educating yourself about sex and sexuality as an adult because you didn't get the information you should have as a child or a teen is both hard and humbling. Again, I cannot more highly recommend availing yourself of the resources available on Scarleteen.com. There is no question you can ask that someone else has not already asked, and it's a lot easier than typing your question into Google and ending up on WebMD being told that your body is abnormal and you're dying.

There are a lot of good resources online, but as we all know, just because you read something online doesn't mean it's true. Start with established organizations, and if you're looking at a smaller site, see if you can find who it's funded or run by. If you're willing, there are also sometimes opportunities for in-person sexuality education for adults. Check and see if any of the churches in your area are offering Our Whole Lives (OWL) workshops (often at Unitarian Universalist and United Church of Christ churches, but not always). Sometimes locally owed sex shops will do sex ed nights where you can learn about various kinds of sex, toys, kinks, and more in a no-shame environment. You might also look at events at the women's or LGBTQ center at any colleges nearby, which are often open to the public as well as students.

Also, for cisgender women specifically, I highly recommend reading *Come as You Are*, the first book by Emily Nagoski, who also cowrote the book *Burnout*, which I quoted at length in chapter 10. *Come as You Are* is an indepth exploration of cisgender women's sexuality and stress response, and it personally transformed the way I think about both.

Where can I find a sex-positive, religiously literate, LGBTQ-affirming therapist that I can afford?

You may think that trying to find a therapist who meets all those qualities is like trying to find a unicorn—and it's not easy. But I've compiled a list of therapists and organizations that understand religious trauma, are affirming of LGBTQ identities, have a sliding scale, and are willing to take clients remotely if needed:

- The Christian Closet
  - Website: thechristiancloset.com
  - Notes: For LGBTQ persons and allies. All service providers charge differently, and not all have a sliding scale, so read the individual bios.
- Cassie McCarty Green
  - Website: rooftopconsulting.com

- Notes: Provides knowledgeable, trauma-informed mental health support for LGBTQ and nonmonogamous folks around the world.
- Laura Anderson and Brian Peck of Religious Trauma Institute
  - Website: religioustraumainstitute.com
  - Notes: As cofounders of Religious Trauma Institute, Laura and Brian are both knowledgeable about the suffering associated with adverse religious experiences (AREs). Their sliding scale availability is limited.
- Reclamation Collective Support Groups
  - Website: reclamationcollective.com
  - Notes: Started by a licensed clinical social worker and a licensed marriage and family therapist who both had adverse experiences with organized Christianity, the Reclamation Collective offers supportive group spaces to navigate religious trauma, spiritual abuse, and faith shifts with a pay-as-you-can model.
- Therapy for Black Girls
  - Website: therapyforblackgirls.com
  - Notes: This website, specifically for Black women, has a searchable database of other Black women therapists and offers both local and virtual options, many of whom accept a broad range of insurance plans. There is also a podcast and a low-cost online community.

Although not necessarily religious, companies like Talk Space (talkspace.com) have many LGBTQ and sex-positive therapists available, take insurance, and offer flexible payment methods. Additionally, you may have local options in your city or town that can be found using Google. The only thing you have to look out for is that oftentimes, counseling groups that offer sliding-scale payment methods are conservative Christian groups that use their affordable therapy as a proselytization method. This is especially true where I live, in the South, but it is something to be aware of no matter where you live. You may have to dig around on their website or call and speak with someone to find out if an organization's counseling comes with a side of evangelism.

Lastly, it may seem like a good idea to have a therapist that comes from a similar religious background as you because they will be able to understand where you're coming from, and that can sometimes be the case—but don't be afraid to branch out. My personal therapist is Jewish, and our difference in religion has been very helpful and enlightening. Sometimes talking about something that *you* think is normal will shock someone of a different background, and it can help to be reminded that the world you came from is just one very small part of the whole world.

How can I start developing a meditation or movement practice?

One thing the wellness industry doesn't want people to know is that developing mindfulness and movement practices is absolutely, 100 percent free. It will always be free to walk, run, take your dog to the park, or roll out your yoga mat at home (and the ten-dollar mat from Target will work just fine—I've been using the same one for three years). If you need some guidance, there's a lot of great free yoga on YouTube. Adriene Mishler (Yoga with Adriene) and Jessamyn

Stanley are two of my favorites. Jessamyn Stanley also wrote a book called *Every Body Yoga* that is a great resource.

If you're white, I also highly recommend listening to the podcast *Yoga Is Dead* by Jesal Parikh and Tejal Patel and following the work of Susanna Barkataki on Instagram. Jesal, Tejal, and Susanna are all women of South Asian descent who teach about the roots of yoga and how it has been colonized and appropriated in Western society to help practitioners of all races practice in a way that respects the heart of yoga and the intentions of the earliest yoga teachers.

Meditation can be as simple as sitting still and observing your thoughts like clouds passing in the sky for one to two minutes. If you're new to meditation, start there and then increase the amount of time gradually. I do most of my meditation before and during my yoga asana practice (asana is the physical postures of yoga), but I have friends who have had great success with the apps Calm and Headspace. I also enjoy the Tara Brach podcast because she has lots of different kinds of meditations of all lengths, and her voice is very soothing.

How do I find a church that supports survivors, LGBTQ folks, women, and other marginalized communities?

Unfortunately, there is no national database (yet) that tracks churches that have mishandled cases of sexual abuse or have protected sexual predators. Denominational efforts to create one, such as the one that has been proposed in the Southern Baptist Church, have been met with little institutional support. And creating a database for just one denomination would stop only a handful of predators if it were implemented at all, since predators often bounce from church to church and from denomination to denomination to avoid the paperwork trail that might give up their game. That's to say nothing of so-called nondenominational churches, like mine in high school, which lack national oversight entirely.

However, with a little time and effort, it is often very easy to find out whether a church is supportive of women, LGBTQ persons, and other marginalized groups and if they support or reject purity culture—before you ever walk through the doors. That won't guarantee they've never harbored a sexual predator or blamed a victim, but it will let you know quite a bit about what they believe about sex and sexuality and how they look at marginalized persons in their community.

The first thing you can do is look them up on churchclarity.org. Church Clarity scores churches based not on their theology but rather on their *clarity* about that theology. You'll be able to see if a church ordains women or allows LGBTQ people to serve in ministry—and whether they are clear or unclear about that policy, which should give you a good indicator of how highly they value honesty and transparency. However, Church Clarity is mostly run by volunteers, so not every church has been scored yet.

If the church you're looking at isn't listed on churchclarity .org, start with the church's website. There's usually a page somewhere titled "Beliefs" or "What We Believe." If a church teaches that men are the head of the household or that marriage is only between a man and a woman, this is usually where they list it. Some churches know how off-putting that kind of retrogressive and harmful theology can be, though, so they won't list it up front. You may have to check out the "Sermons" page or the pastor's blog to get a good sense of what they really believe. See if you can find pictures of the church's activities. Notice who is present and who is absent. Notice who is leading activities and who is following. Also, double-check if the church has their abuse policy or any information pertaining to child safety posted on their website.

Many churches will never make the changes required of them in order to stop being a force for net harm in the world, and therefore I believe they should die off. However, I have also experienced firsthand the healing power of positive faith community, and I do believe that there are churches out there that are doing the work in order to make themselves safe and sexually just spaces for survivors. It's just up to survivors to determine whether they are succeeding in that endeavor—not church leaders or committees or denominational governing bodies.

If I have a #ChurchToo story, how do I come forward publicly?

Whether or not to share your story publicly is a deeply personal and intimate decision that no one should ever be pressured into. If it's something you want to do, you have options. Using the #ChurchToo hashtag online is a good way to get your story in front of lots of people quickly and is especially effective on Twitter and Instagram. There are also multiple websites where you can create a free blog without much knowledge of coding or website design if you want to share your story in a long-form format.

Into Account has a form on their website that you can use to share your story and request support. You can find it by visiting intoaccount.org and clicking "Submit a Report." The form will ask you some questions about your experience and give you space to share details, and there is a box you can check if you'd like help publicizing your story.

If you still live in the area where your story took place, local newspapers and other local publications are a good bet if you can get a hold of a specific journalist. You can even reach out if you don't live there anymore; it is just usually easier to start with small local publications rather than national news media outlets.

Just know that when you come forward publicly, people will ask you a lot of very specific questions about what happened to you, usually over and over. It is a process that is not for the faint of heart, and it's important to take care of yourself, drink water, take breaks, and know that you can always take a step back if you need to. The fiftieth time you tell your story is definitely easier than the first, but it never really gets *easy*. Know that if you come forward, no matter how many people see your story, you are brave for speaking up and sharing your truth, and nobody can ever take that away from you.

NOTES

Introduction

1. Laura Anderson, @lauraandersontherapy, Instagram, October 25, 2019, accessed April 7, 2020. https://tinyurl.com/y3pa9ero.

Chapter 1

1. Emma Zyriek, Facebook, accessed September 28, 2019, https://tinyurl.com/y2xwqye5.
2. Randall Balmer, "The Real Origins of the Religious Right," Politico, accessed September 28, 2019, https://tinyurl.com/y3x46nzj.
3. Balmer.
4. Fred Clark, "White Evangelicalism Is White Nationalism," Patheos, accessed September 28, 2019, https://tinyurl.com/y4wq2cbp.
5. Clark.
6. True Love Waits, "History," LifeWay, accessed September 28, 2019, https://tinyurl.com/y475qybq.
7. Peter Lewis Allen, *The Wages of Sin: Sex and Disease, Past and Present* (Chicago: University of Chicago Press, 2000), reproduced in Allen, "The Birth of the Helms Amendment: How a Single Pamphlet Started an AIDS War," FindLaw.com, accessed September 30, 2019, https://tinyurl.com/y6dqcfqe.
8. Hans Johnson and William Eskridge, "The Legacy of Falwell's Bully Pulpit," *Washington Post*, May 19, 2007, accessed September 30, 2019, https://tinyurl.com/y4vasjkx.
9. Allen, *Wages of Sin*.

10. "Timeline of Abstinence-Only Education in U.S. Classrooms," National Coalition against Censorship, accessed September 30, 2019, https://tinyurl.com/yy24ykxk.

11. "Timeline."

12. See Donna Freitas, *Sex and the Soul: Juggling Sexuality, Spirituality, Romance and Religion on America's College Campuses* (Oxford: Oxford University Press, 2008); and Jessica Valenti, *The Purity Myth: How America's Obsession with Virginity Is Hurting Young Women* (Berkeley: Seal, 2009).

13. Julie Beck, "The Concept Creep of Emotional Labor," *Atlantic*, November 26, 2018, accessed September 30, 2019, https://tinyurl.com/yxqq4btg.

14. Joe Carter, "The FAQs: What You Should Know about Purity Culture," Gospel Coalition, July 24, 2019, accessed September 30, 2019, https://tinyurl.com/y428hruo.

15. Brené Brown and Jan Fleury, "Shame versus Guilt—Brené Brown," YouTube video, September 21, 2015, accessed May 21, 2020, https://www.youtube.com/watch?v=DqGFrId-IQg.

16. Matthias Roberts, *Beyond Shame: Creating a Healthy Sex Life on Your Own Terms* (Minneapolis: Fortress, 2020), 19.

17. Roberts, 25.

18. Linda Kay Klein, *Pure: Inside the Evangelical Movement That Shamed a Generation of Young Women and How I Broke Free* (New York: Touchstone, 2018), 14.

19. Laura Anderson, "'He Said, She Said' with Ashley Spivey," *Reality Steve Podcast*, episode 20, July 30, 2019, accessed October 8, 2019.

20. Robert Downen, Lise Olsen, and John Tedesco, "20 Years, 700 Victims: Southern Baptist Sexual Abuse Spreads as Leaders Resist Reforms," *Houston Chronicle*, February 10, 2019, accessed April 13, 2020, https://tinyurl.com/y4wx3fqh.

Chapter 2

1. Kate Shellnut, "Report: How Southern Baptists Failed to Care about Abuse," *Christianity Today*, June 10, 2019, accessed October 10, 2019, https://tinyurl.com/y6rag7om.

2. Justin Lookadoo, who went on to have a famed career as an abstinence-only speaker and entertainer after the publication of

Dateable, was arrested and charged with public intoxication in 2014.

3. Justin Lookadoo and Hayley Morgan, *Dateable: Are You? Are They?* (Grand Rapids: Flemming H. Revell, 2003), 109–10.

4. *Fat* is the term Charlotte told me she prefers when talking about herself.

5. Shannon Ethridge and Stephen Arterburn, *Every Young Woman's Battle: Guarding Your Mind, Heart, and Body in a Sex-Saturated World* (Colorado Springs: Waterbrook, 2004), 92.

6. Ethridge and Arterburn, 90.

7. Jessica Valenti, *The Purity Myth: How America's Obsession with Virginity Is Hurting Young Women* (Berkeley: Seal, 2009), 147.

Chapter 3

1. James K. A. Smith, *The Fall of Interpretation: Philosophical Foundations for a Creational Hermeneutic* (Grand Rapids: Baker Academic, 2000).

2. Joshua Harris, *I Kissed Dating Goodbye: A New Attitude toward Romance and Relationships* (Colorado Springs: Multnomah, 1997).

3. Joshua Harris, @harrisjosh, Instagram, July 17, 2019, accessed July 19, 2020, https://www.instagram.com/p/B0CtVRingGj/.

4. Ted Olsen, "As Appeal Is Announced in Sovereign Grace Case, Joshua Harris Says He Was Abused as a Child," *Christianity Today*, May 20, 2013, accessed October 26, 2019, https://tinyurl.com/y4kuqf98.

5. In 2017, Harris released the documentary *I Survived "I Kissed Dating Goodbye,"* where he spoke to many of those affected by his work. The documentary had mixed reception, as it featured several purity culture celebrities and abstinence-only peddlers and presented their statements in a positive way. In 2019, Harris began apologizing more explicitly via Instagram, announcing that he was no longer a Christian and apologizing for the way his work harmed the LGBTQ community specifically.

6. Michelle Boorstein, "Pastor Joshua Harris, an Evangelical Outlier, Heads to Mainstream Seminary," *Washington Post*, January 30, 2015, accessed October 26, 2019.

7. Eric Ludy and Leslie Ludy, *When God Writes Your Love Story* (Colorado Springs: Multnomah, 1999), 84.

8. Shannon Ethridge and Stephen Arterburn, *Every Young Woman's Battle: Guarding Your Mind, Heart, and Body in a Sex-Saturated World* (Colorado Springs: Waterbrook, 2004), 21.

9. Mary A. Kassian, *Girls Gone Wise in a World Gone Wild* (Chicago: Moody, 2010), 144.

10. Noël Clark, "The Etiology and Phenomenology of Sexual Shame: A Grounded Study Theory" (PhD diss., Seattle Pacific University, 2017).

11. Clark, 87.

Chapter 4

1. Church Clarity is a crowdsourced database of Christian churches that encourages churches to be clear about their actively enforced policies regarding women and LGBTQ persons in the leadership and life of the church. Visit churchclarity.org to learn more.

2. "Student Life Guide 2019–2020," Moody Bible Institute, 2019, accessed September 14, 2019. https://tinyurl.com/y58gu7rj.

3. Esther Eaton, "Moody Bible Institute Promises Investigation of Abuse Complaints," *World Magazine*, October 29, 2020, https://tinyurl.com/y3dbrguk.

4. "Student Handbook 2020–2021," University of Valley Forge, 2020, accessed July 19, 2020, 14, https://tinyurl.com/yxjlfj42.

5. "Undergraduate Student Handbook and Guide to University Policies," Biola University, 2015, accessed September 14, 2019, 6, https://tinyurl.com/y3fzn8fu.

6. "Press on to Maturity Student Handbook 2019–2010," Florida College, 2019, accessed September 14, 2019, 7, https://tinyurl.com/y5c8n5wr.

7. "Bryan Community Standards," Bryan College, accessed September 14, 2019, 3, https://tinyurl.com/yyysmpq9.

8. "Student Handbook 2019–2020," Bob Jones University, 2019, accessed November 11, 2019, 63, http://www.bju.edu/life-faith/student-handbook.pdf.

9. "The Liberty Way," Liberty University, accessed July 19, 2020, 14–15. This document is publicly unavailable but was sent to me by a former student.

10. Emily McFarlan Miller, "The Fall of Falwell: A Timeline of the Ups, Downs and Scandals of His Liberty University Presidency," Religion News Service, August 25, 2020, https://tinyurl .com/y4j7t96u.

11. Brandon Ambrosino, "'She Was the Aggressor': Former Liberty Student Alleges Sexual Encounter with Becki Falwell," Politico, August 27, 2020, https://tinyurl.com/y62lygfj.

12. Joshua Harris, *I Kissed Dating Goodbye: A New Attitude toward Romance and Relationships* (Colorado Springs: Multnomah, 1997), 90.

13. Hilary Jerome Scarsella, "When Sexual Violence Happens in the Church: Questions to Prompt Reflection on Your Community's Preparedness," Into Account, 2018, presented at the Alliance of Baptists' Just Sex Conference, Vanderbilt University, Nashville, Tennessee, September 2018.

14. Julia's name and the names of others in this story have been changed.

15. Complementarianism is the theological belief that men and women are equal in value but different in what roles they are allowed to fill at home, in church, and in society. I'll discuss it more in chapter 8.

Chapter 5

1. Elizabeth Smart, Comments to John Hopkins University, May 1, 2013, clip cited in John Oliver, "Sex Education: *Last Week Tonight with John Oliver*," YouTube video, HBO, August 9, 2015, https:// tinyurl.com/y4dtahsb.

2. Oliver, "Sex Education."

3. "State Policies on Sex Education in Schools," National Conference of State Legislatures, March 21, 2019, accessed November 23, 2019, https://tinyurl.com/m5gd7f6.

4. Josh McDowell, *How to Help Your Children Say "No" to Sexual Pressure* (Waco, TX: Word, 1987), 21.

5. Shellie R. Warren, *Pure Heart: A Woman's Guide to Sexual Integrity* (Grand Rapids: Baker, 2010), 39.

6. "Sex Addiction," Healthline.com, accessed November 23, 2019, https://www.healthline.com/health/addiction/sex.

7.   Shannon Ethridge and Stephen Arterburn, *Every Young Woman's Battle: Guarding Your Mind, Heart, and Body in a Sex-Saturated World* (Colorado Springs: Waterbrook, 2004), 167.

8.   Dannah Gresh and Juli Slattery, *Pulling Back the Shades: Erotica, Intimacy, and the Longings of a Woman's Heart* (Chicago: Moody, 2014), 37.

9.   Ethridge and Arterburn, *Every Young Woman's Battle*, 168.

10.   "About," Heritage Foundation, accessed November 23, 2019, https://www.heritage.org/about-heritage/mission.

11.   "Research Brief: Accepting Adults Reduce Suicide Attempts among LGBTQ Youth," Trevor Project, June 27, 2019, accessed December 8, 2019, https://tinyurl.com/y3gg6trf.

12.   Shelly Donahue, clip cited in Oliver, "Sex Education."

13.   "When Does Life Begin?," Life Matters Worldwide, accessed November 23, 2019, https://tinyurl.com/y3fjw2sd.

14.   Rachel Benson Gold, "The Implications of Defining When a Woman Is Pregnant," Guttmacher Institute, May 9, 2005, accessed April 20, 2020, https://tinyurl.com/yyhrky59.

15.   It's also worth noting that scientists tend to use the word *conception* to refer to implantation, whereas pro-life advocates tend to use it to refer to fertilization. This differentiation becomes very salient when pro-life advocates argue against certain forms of birth control, such as IUDs, claiming that they are "abortifacients" because they believe they could potentially interfere with a fertilized egg's implantation.

16.   Ethridge and Arterburn, *Every Young Woman's Battle*, 176.

17.   Gresh and Slattery, *Pulling Back the Shades*, 34.

18.   Heather Corinna, "Sex Education Can Stop Abuse," *Guardian*, April 30, 2019, accessed November 24, 2019, https://tinyurl.com/y5z8n53z.

19.   McDowell, *How to Help Your Children*, 35–36.

20.   Homeschool co-ops are gatherings of homeschooling families where children are able to get together and take classes from different parents with expertise in different subjects as a way for families to share resources and build community.

Chapter 6

1. Miguel A. De La Torre, *A Lily among the Thorns: Imagining a New Christian Sexuality* (San Francisco: Jossey-Bass, 2007), 131.
2. HRC Staff, "New Report on Youth Homeless Affirms That LGBTQ Youth Disproportionately Experience Homelessness," HRC.org, November 15, 2017, accessed December 8, 2019, https://tinyurl.com/ya7pn9wy.
3. Annie Shearer et al., "Differences in Mental Health Symptoms across Lesbian, Gay, Bisexual, and Questioning Youth in Primary Care Settings," *Journal of Adolescent Health* 59, no. 1 (July 2016): 38–43, accessed December 8, 2019, https://tinyurl.com/y375xcab.
4. Tim LaHaye, *The Unhappy Gays: What Everyone Should Know about Homosexuality* (Carol Stream, IL: Tyndale House, 1978), 57–58.
5. "Research Brief: Accepting Adults Reduce Suicide Attempts among LGBTQ Youth," Trevor Project, June 27, 2019, accessed December 8, 2019, https://tinyurl.com/y3gg6trf.
6. Brian Murphy and Shannon T. L. Kearns, "No, QCF, It's Not 'Possible to Have a Healthy Relationship with Your Child' If You Don't Affirm Them," Queer Theology, March 27, 2019, accessed December 8, 2019, https://tinyurl.com/y4c7t4qu.

Chapter 7

1. *Ethical nonmonogamy* refers to romantic or sexual relationships wherein partners agree that they are able to form romantic or sexual relationships with other people with the full knowledge of all parties involved.
2. Franklin Veaux and Eve Rickert, *More Than Two: A Practical Guide to Ethical Polyamory* (Portland: Thorntree Press, 2014), 41. It should be noted that Franklin Veaux has had his own share of allegations of sexual misconduct and other forms of abuse come to light in recent years, and those looking to learn more about ethical nonmonogamy or polyamory should engage his work with caution.
3. And by the way, the exception for abuse isn't necessarily "biblical," strictly speaking. The bible carves out explicit exceptions for cheating and abandonment by someone who is not a Christian,

but the abuse exception is one that most Christian communities will also accept because to not do so would make them appear extremely cruel.

4. John Piper, "John Piper: Does a Woman Submit to Abuse?," eaandfath, YouTube video, September 1, 2009, accessed December 10, 2019, https://www.youtube.com/watch?v=3OkUPc2NLrM.

5. Bob Allen, "Man Confesses to Child Porn; Church Disciplines His Wife," *Baptist News Global,* May 29, 2015, accessed December 10, 2019, https://tinyurl.com/y6fj58gb.

6. Names have been changed in this story.

7. "Biblical counseling" is a type of counseling in which only the bible is used rather than therapeutic systems or psychological knowledge. Biblical counselors exist outside of the accreditation network through which legitimate counselors and therapists get certified and are usually not credentialed therapists unless they have received additional training elsewhere. Biblical counseling is different than Christian counseling or religious counseling in general.

8. Peter Jankowski et al., "Religious Beliefs and Domestic Violence Myths," *Psychology of Religion and Spirituality* 10, no. 4 (March 22, 2018): 386–97.

9. Jankowski, 386.

10. Jankowski, 387.

11. Jankowski, 388.

12. Jankowski, 393.

Chapter 8

1. *The Danvers Statement,* Council on Biblical Manhood and Womanhood, November 1988, accessed January 2, 2019, https://cbmw.org/about/danvers-statement/.

2. Depending on who you ask, the relationship between men and women in complementarianism is also meant to imitate the interrelating of the members of the Trinity or the Godhead, where Jesus submits to God the Father eternally even though they are equal in value. This is an interesting and inexplicably non-Arian heresy known as "eternal subordination," and it's gained a lot of popularity among evangelicals, especially since the

beginning of the modern purity movement and the resurgence of
neo-Calvinism.

3. Jonathan Parnell, "When the Sex Should Stop," *Desiring God* blog,
    November 14, 2013, accessed January 4, 2020, https://tinyurl
    .com/yyqedhzg.

4. Ed Stetzer, "All Faith Groups, Evangelicals Included, Need to
    Reflect on #MeToo," *Christianity Today*, December 12, 2018,
    accessed January 4, 2020, https://tinyurl.com/yyr74awv.

5. Becca Andrews, "As a Teen, Emily Joy Was Abused by a Church
    Youth Leader. Now She's Leading a Movement to Change Evan-
    gelical America," *Mother Jones*, May 25, 2018, accessed Decem-
    ber 30, 2019, https://tinyurl.com/ycm4qqpo.

6. The following is the actual quote from former pastor Andy
    Savage referenced in the *Mother Jones* article: "I was encouraged
    by what's coming out of the #MeToo movement, the sense of
    seeking a balanced voice. I feel like the #ChurchToo movement,
    what little I've seen and what's been related to me, is that there's
    not a real effort to seek a balanced voice in terms of all sides of the
    issue. It feels, at least from my perspective, it feels very aggressive
    and very attacking."

7. Bill Gothard is the founder and leader of the Christian home-
    schooling cult Institute in Basic Life Principles. He famously pop-
    ularized the graphic called the "Umbrella of Protection," featuring
    three umbrellas, with Christ over the husband, the husband over
    the wife, and finally, the wife over the children. He has been
    accused of sexual harassment and assault by over thirty women.

8. Robert Downen et al., "Abuse of Faith: 20 Years, 700 Vic-
    tims: Southern Baptist Sexual Abuse Spreads as Leaders Resist
    Reforms," *Houston Chronicle*, February 10, 2019, accessed Janu-
    ary 1, 2020, https://tinyurl.com/y4wx3fqh.

9. In February 2020, in response to the #MeToo and #ChurchToo
    movements, the Southern Baptist Convention (SBC) for the first
    time in its history expelled a church in Midland, Texas, that was
    pastored by a man who was convicted of sexually assaulting an
    eleven-year-old girl and a twelve-year-old girl. The Texas church
    was not the only church considered for removal, and others
    that had been submitted for consideration included the church
    where Jules was abused. However, no action was taken by the
    SBC at that time to censure or expel other churches. The SBC
    blamed their lack of action on other reported churches not having
    gone through their full inquiry process. Robert Downen, "Texas

Church with Sex Offender Pastor First to Be Ousted under SBC Abuse Reforms," *Houston Chronicle*, February 18, 2020, accessed April 8, 2020, https://tinyurl.com/y6o6eyaj.

10. Daphne Eck et al., "Let's Talk about Chris Heuertz," Medium, June 10, 2020, accessed October 8, 2020, https://tinyurl.com/y6d5nebw.

Chapter 9

1. Thabiti Anyabwile, "The Importance of Your Gag Reflex When Discussing Homosexuality and 'Gay Marriage,'" Gospel Coalition, August 19, 2013, accessed January 9, 2020, https://tinyurl.com/yxaa9yjv.

2. Interview with Pelican Project members Karen Swallow Prior, Kristie Anyabwile, and Tish Harrison Warren, "A New Guild Aims to Equip Women and Amplify Orthodoxy," *Christianity Today*, November 2018, accessed January 9, 2020, https://tinyurl.com/y5rsamaa.

3. This observation should be credited to my fiancée, Caitlin, who pointed it out to me when we were discussing my ideas for this chapter.

4. Emily Nagoski and Amelia Nagoski, *Burnout: The Secret to Unlocking the Stress Cycle* (New York: Ballantine, 2019).

5. Kate Manne, *Down Girl: The Logic of Misogyny* (New York: Oxford University Press, 2017).

6. Nagoski and Nagoski, *Burnout*, xiii.

7. Nagoski and Nagoski, xiii–xiv.

8. Miguel A. De La Torre, *A Lily among the Thorns: Imagining a New Christian Sexuality* (San Francisco: Jossey-Bass, 2007), 39.

9. Nagoski and Nagoski, *Burnout*, xiv.

10. "Victims of Sexual Violence: Statistics," Rape, Abuse, and Incest National Network (RAINN), accessed January 18, 2020, https://www.rainn.org/statistics/victims-sexual-violence.

11. @darcorina, Twitter, November 21, 2017, 10:46 PM, https://tinyurl.com/y4s4lcud.

12. @LindaKayKlein, Twitter, November 28, 2017, 9:11 AM, https://tinyurl.com/y4a9poy7. The text of this tweet has been slightly edited for publication at the request of its author.

13. The author of this tweet requested that their handle be anonymous.

14. @DaisyRainMartin, Twitter, September 21, 2018, 9:50 PM, https://tinyurl.com/y2wwuqc8.

15. @ThatMandyNicole, Twitter, November 23, 2017, 2:48 PM, https://tinyurl.com/y37ulhr7.

16. @mandster60, Twitter, November 26, 2017, 8:52 AM, https://tinyurl.com/yywmx52z.

17. @bougiefeminist, Twitter, November 23, 2017, 9:59 PM, https://tinyurl.com/y3wfzokw.

18. @lilmermaidtiff, Twitter, November 22, 2017, 10:14 PM, https://tinyurl.com/y2khpvc5.

19. Sarah Pulliam Bailey, "Southern Baptist Leader Encouraged a Woman Not to Report Alleged Rape and Told Her to Forgive Assailant, She Says," *Washington Post*, May 22, 2018, accessed January 20, 2020, https://tinyurl.com/y7hw3x26.

20. Bailey.

21. Michelle Boorstein, "Southern Baptist Leader Pushes Back after Comments Leak Urging Abused Women to Pray and Avoid Divorce," *Washington Post*, April 29, 2018, accessed January 20, 2020, https://tinyurl.com/y89bnzzc.

Chapter 10

1. For resources on how to let go of purity culture completely when you still have theological misgivings or are a part of a community that is not ready to have these conversations, see the appendix in the back of the book.

2. *Parks and Recreation*, season 5, episode 4, "Sex Education," directed by Craig Zisk, written by Alan Yang, NBC 2012, October 18, 2012.

3. Bessel Van der Kolk, *The Body Keeps the Score: Brain, Mind, and Body in the Healing of Trauma* (New York: Penguin, 2014), 74–88.

4. Glennon Doyle's description of her first hot yoga class in her book *Love Warrior* is pretty much exactly how I feel about yoga and doing hard things and should be required reading for everybody considering going to their first hot yoga class or really any yoga class at all.

5. Van der Kolk, *Body Keeps the Score*, 82.
6. The phrase "cornucopia of trauma" comes from the television show *Schitt's Creek*, from the character Moira Rose, played by the inimitable Catherine O'Hara.
7. Sophie Khadr et al., "Mental and Sexual Health Outcomes following Sexual Assault in Adolescents: A Prospective Cohort Study," *Lancet Child and Adolescent Health* 2, no. 9 (2018): 654–65, accessed February 1, 2020, https://doi.org/10.1016/S2352-4642(18)30202 -5.
8. "Victims of Sexual Violence: Statistics," Rape, Abuse and Incest National Network (RAINN), accessed February 1, 2020, https:// tinyurl.com/hpwax6p.

Conclusion

1. Anne Lamott, @ANNELAMOTT, Twitter, April 23, 2012, 8:16 PM, https://tinyurl.com/yyrgbp9n.
2. The idea of women as "moral children" comes from Jessica Valenti in *The Purity Myth*.
3. Matthew McKay, Jeffrey Wood, and Jeffrey Brantley, *The Dialectical Behavior Therapy Skills Workbook: Practical DBT Exercises for Learning Mindfulness, Interpersonal Effectiveness, Emotion Regulation and Distress Tolerance* (Oakland, CA: New Harbinger, 2007), 51.
4. McKay, Wood, and Brantley, 51.